# CONTENTS

# CAESAR
## AND THE
# CHURCH

*A BIBLICAL STUDY OF*
*GOVERNMENT AND CHURCH*

ANTHONY FORSYTH

KRESS
BIBLICAL
RESOURCES

# PREFACE

I am writing this towards the end of 2021. The world has been dramatically impacted by COVID-19 and, more so, the various responses to it. In many countries, governments mandated restrictions in society at large that also spilled over into churches. Churches, in various places and at various times, were told to meet outdoors, to wear masks, to socially distance, to refrain from singing, and even to cancel services altogether. Initially, we were told this was a temporary measure - "fifteen days to flatten the curve" - and that it was necessary solely to lessen the burden on medical services. Over a year and a half later, many of us are still living under the same restrictions.

The response from churches and their leaders has been incredibly varied. Some shut down and still haven't reopened other than through live streaming, while at the other end of the spectrum, some have rejected the mandates and have met as normal throughout this time. There is no doubt a church out there somewhere to fit into every possible position between those two extremes. In short, there are churches that have done everything that Caesar has asked, and there are churches that have rejected all of his mandates, often with serious repercussions. Now we even have churches that have banned those who are unvaccinated.

One thing has been clear from the start: that most churches, and most Christians, did not have a well thought out and previously established theology on these matters. That is hardly surprising - most people in "legacy brand" countries have not experienced their governments imposing any restrictions on church services at all. Whereas in times gone by, the conflict between church and state resulted in church leaders having a robust biblical position on such matters since World War II has been in the rearview mirror, the church has had little pressing need to consider such matters at all.

In this small volume, I seek to present a biblical understanding of government, its God-given role, and specifically how it interacts with and impacts the Church. I am writing as a Bible-believing Christian to other Bible-believing Christians. I presume that the reader not only believes that the Bible is inerrant (without error), authoritative (we must do what it says), and sufficient (it contains all that is needed to live godly lives), but also, that he wants to be instructed by it on how to navigate these strange times. In short, we want to know what the Bible says regarding our interactions with Caesar because we love God, love His Word, and want to obey Him, whatever the cost.

This is not a book about COVID-19 - for I am not a doctor. This is not a book about the U.S. Constitution - after all, I'm not a lawyer nor even American. This is simply for God's people everywhere. It is simply one pastor's attempt to clearly articulate the Bible's teaching on authority in government and specifically how that impacts the bride of Christ. I have not sought to be comprehensive but rather opted for brevity and accessibility. I want to make the Bible's teaching understandable to the reader so that their decision-making might be built on biblical foundations.

I trust that, in God's hands, it may do just that.

# ACKNOWLEDGEMENTS AND DEDICATION

My thinking on this topic has developed significantly over the last few years. I won't pretend that the view I hold now is exactly what I believed two years ago. To be honest, I hadn't really worked through these issues in significant depth until I was forced to. I am thankful for the many who challenged me to think through these issues and whose thinking has impacted my own, especially Andrew Smith, Bud Ahlheim, Herald Gandi, Kofi Adu-Boahen, Matthew Trewhella, Mike Riccardi, Rochadd Hendrix, Tim Moen, and especially Chris Le Duc.

I will forever be grateful to John MacArthur for the stance he took and the boldness with which he stood, providing cover for smaller local churches such as ours who were also seeking to be faithful under fire. Those who are now enjoying meeting indoors in California are doing so, without threat, thanks to his actions and those of other brave leaders. I also want to acknowledge the faithful walk of men like James Coates and Tim Stephens, who obeyed God rather than men, even to the point of imprisonment.

Many have cast their eye on this work during its development and have provided useful feedback and corrections - grammatical, practical, and theological. Thanks to Bud Ahlheim, Chris Le Duc, Cory Marsh, David K Martin, Jenny Forsyth, Kofi Adu-Boahen, Obadiah MacAdoo, Rick Kress, Rochadd Hendrix, Sara Moen, and Tim Moen. All mistakes and errors are, of course, my own.

But most of all, I want to thank my wife, Jenny, without whom this book would not be here. She not only encouraged me and helped me to get this done, but she also stood by me faithfully for 25 years in good times and bad, holding me up when I was too weak to stand alone.

It is to her and to her faithful love that I dedicate this book.

*"The things of God are not subject to the authority of the emperor."*

AMBROSE, *Letter 20*, 385 A.D.

*"For tyranny is abuse of power entrusted by God to man."*
JOHN OF SALISBURY, *The Statesman's Book*, 12th century

*"Human law, when it does not agree with the divine, is unjust."*
MARTIN LUTHER

*"Though the partisans of arbitrary power will freely censure that preacher who speaks boldly for the liberties of the people, they will admire as an excellent divine, the parson whose discourse is wholly in the opposite, and teaches, that magistrates have a divine right for doing wrong, and are to be implicitly obeyed; men professing Christianity, as if the religion of the blessed Jesus bound them to bow their neck to any tyrant."*

WILLIAM GORDON, *Sermon*, 1794

*"The greatest protection which we may take against the destructive doctrine of the absolute sovereignty of the State is the doctrine of the sovereignty of God. Only God is sovereign in all spheres of life and has decreed the limits of State and Church jurisdictions. God is sovereign over the individual conscience, not the State. The State is the servant of God and not the master of men."*

MARCELLUS KIK, *Church & State*, 1963

# Introduction

*"Every person is to be in subjection to the governing authorities. For there is no authority except from God, and those which exist have been appointed by God.*

*Therefore, whoever resists that authority has opposed the ordinance of God; and they who have opposed will receive condemnation upon themselves.*

*For rulers are not a cause of fear for good behavior, but for evil. Do you want to have no fear of that authority? Do what is good, and you will have praise from the same;*

*for it is a minister of God to you for good. But if you do what is evil, be afraid; for it does not bear the sword in vain, for it is a minister of God, an avenger who brings wrath on the one who practices evil."* ROMANS 13:1-4

# The Bone of Contention

We all have the same Bible (albeit in the form of different translations) and the same text. Yet, over the last few years, as churches have sought to respond biblically to restrictions placed upon them by various forms of government, the responses have been astonishingly different.

Some churches have responded to Caesar's impositions with a resounding "No" in the face of threats, fines, and even imprisonment. Others have responded to Caesar's command to jump with "how high?" Both would doubtless consider themselves as being biblical in their decisions - seeking to be obedient to God. If we're honest, we could probably find a church to fit every possible position in between these polar extremes.

## ONE INTERPRETATION

The great irony is that the standard theological position of most Bible-believing churches is the same, even though the practical outworking has been vastly different.

A contemporary trend, perilous to the proper interpretation and subsequent application of Scripture, is that many Christians primarily deal with Bible verses in isolation. A verse is quoted on a card, on a mug, on a social media post. So when Romans 13:1a says, "Every person is to be in subjection to the governing authorities," for most Christians, this is a slam dunk. We are commanded to submit to the government, so we must. Always. The only exception would be if the commands of government were sinful - if obedience to Caesar were to cause us to be disobedient to God. 1 Peter 2:13-14 and Titus 3:1 seem to say the same thing, and so it is a simple open and shut case. We might summarize that interpretation as "Obey Caesar apart from sin." Though it is merely an opinion based on limited observation, I suspect that the vast majority of Bible-believing Christians held this view pre-COVID, and even now, most still do. It was curious to see that the subsequent decisions made by churches who agreed on that interpretation have varied hugely. I would suggest that there are two main reasons for that.

## Two Different Definitions

The two different reasons both boil down to how we are defining our terms. Firstly, while there is an agreement in the interpretation "Obey Caesar apart from sin," there is disagreement over who Caesar is.

In America, for example, it is often noted that the highest authority of the land is the Constitution. This document is "Caesar" for Americans and not a person at all. All other government leaders from the police up to the president are subject to this document as the rule of law and must swear an oath to uphold it. If somebody makes a rule, issues a mandate, or signs an executive order that is in contradiction to the Constitution then, it is argued, that rule is not legally valid. But even if that were the case (and interpretation of the Constitution is highly divergent in this nation), does one reject that rule immediately, or does one have to wait until a case is made through various courts until finally, the Supreme Court makes a ruling? Regardless, this principle has been the basis for churches rejecting mandates handed down by lower authorities from mayors to governors, even to the president.

While the U.S. Constitution stands alone in its uniqueness, some other legacy brand countries have similar charters, although many do not. This American application thus often has the effect of brushing aside the situation of other nations.

While there may be agreement that one must submit to Caesar, that does not give us full agreement on to whom exactly we must submit. Do we submit to every law enforcement officer? To the governor? To the city mayor? To the local health authority? To the CDC or the WHO? Or simply to the Constitution alone? What does the Christian do if some of these authorities disagree with each other? Who decides whether a particular interpretation of a law is correct? These complications only increase when we consider various forms of government in different nations.

Secondly, even if one agrees to submit (and agrees with regards to whom or what precisely we must submit to), there is the universally accepted exception - commands that cause us to sin. The trouble here is that as much as there is disagreement on whom to submit to, there has often been as much disagreement on which commands are, in fact, sinful. Is resorting to live stream only services a rejection of Hebrews 10:24-25 and the exhortation not to neglect meeting together, or is Zoom, in fact, in this media-friendly culture, a legitimate form of meeting together? Is a mandate forbidding singing a step too far, or is singing in our hearts an unwelcome restriction but one that does not lead us to sin and thus one that must be obeyed?

And so, despite a majority view on what the text actually means, there is a huge disparity and often very vigorous disputation on what its application should look like in our current situation.

Clearly, we urgently need clarity on what the Bible teaches on this matter generally and on this passage in particular. Either some have bowed to Caesar erroneously, thinking that in doing so, they have also bowed to Christ, or else others have rebelled against God while rebelling against Caesar. Some people may have done both at different times and in different ways. This issue is serious and must be resolved biblically.

## ANOTHER INTERPRETATION

Let me say this clearly from the beginning: I believe that such an interpretation of Romans 13, though by far the majority view, is incorrect, regardless of how one defines "Caesar" or "sin."

Our tendency to take a verse in isolation leads so often to an overly simplistic and frequently inaccurate interpretation of the text. If we are to be mature believers, with the Word of Christ dwelling in us richly (Col 3:16), we must go beyond a superficial understanding of Scripture founded merely on a few isolated verses. Such shallowness will often lead to incorrect understandings of the authorial intent of Scripture.

Christians have often responded to any debate on this issue with a summary dismissal and the cry of "Romans 13!" No need to discuss further - Scripture has spoken!

As such, it is necessary for us to engage in a detailed study of Romans 13, in particular its connections to the context of Romans 12, if we are to understand Paul's (and God's) intent. But before we get there, we must look at an even broader context - the context of Scripture as a whole. What does the Bible say about authority generally? To whom does God give authority, and what does that entail practically? This will provide us with a broad foundation for rightly considering Romans 13.

*"First, the Holy Scripture does teach that God reigns by his own proper authority and kings by derivation, God from Himself, kings from God, that God hath a jurisdiction proper, kings are His delegates. It follows then that the jurisdiction of God hath no limits, that of kings bounded; that the power of God is infinite, that of kings confined; that the kingdom of God extends itself to all places, that of kings is restrained within the confines of certain countries."*
JUNIUS BRUTUS, *Vindiciae Contra Tyrannos: A Defense Of Liberty Against Tyrants,* 1579

*"The sphere of the church is distinct from that of the civil magistrate … What needs to be appreciated now is that its sphere is co-ordinate with that of the state. The church is not subordinate to the state, nor is the state subordinate to the church. They are both subordinate to God …when the civil magistrate trespasses the limits of his authority, it is incumbent upon the church to expose and condemn such a violation of his authority."*
JOHN MURRAY, *Collected Writings,* 1950s

*"No totalitarian authority nor authoritarian state can tolerate those who have an absolute by which to judge that state and its actions."*
*"If there are no absolutes by which to judge society, then society becomes an absolute."*
FRANCIS SCHAEFFER, *How Shall We Then Live?,* 1976

*"Three main social spheres are designed by God: family, church, and state. The state is restricted and is not to be an all-expansive leviathan, reaching its tentacles into every possible compartment where the citizen will permit. If one understands the sovereignty of God, one sees that the state has delegated tasks and serves according to his plan; it should be structured accordingly. However, the state must never see itself as sovereign, lest it fall into idolatry. The state is not free to write its own charter, but must bow the knee to the true sovereign Creator of the state."*
DAVID W. HALL, *Savior or Servant? Putting Government In Its Place,* 2020

# Part One

## Biblical Foundations and Principles

"In the beginning, God created the heavens and the earth." GENESIS 1:1

"And Jesus came up and spoke to them, saying, "All authority has been given to Me in heaven and on earth.

Go therefore and make disciples of all the nations, baptizing them in the name of the Father and the Son and the Holy Spirit,

teaching them to keep all that I commanded you; and behold, I am with you always, even to the end of the age." MATTHEW 28:18-20

"'You have put all things in subjection under his feet.'

For in subjecting all things to him, He left nothing that is not subject to him. But now we do not yet see all things subjected to him." HEBREWS 2:8

"For in Him all things were created, both in the heavens and on earth, visible and invisible, whether thrones or dominions or rulers or authorities— all things have been created through Him and for Him." COLOSSIANS 1:16

# 1

## ALL AUTHORITY IS GOD'S

That all authority belongs to God is the most basic principle. It is one that should not even need to be stated, let alone argued, amongst Christians. God in Christ not only created everything in both the heavens and on earth (John 1:3) but they were created for Him (Col 1:16). In short, He made everything. Everything is His. He's in charge. Period. All authority is God's.

Christ has been given all authority (Matt 28:18), and so He can command the disciples to go and make disciples with the expectation of obedience. Although it may not look like it when we see ungodly leaders around the world, everything is subject to Him (Heb 2:8). He is seated at the right hand of the Father in Heaven, even if He does not yet sit on His Davidic throne upon the earth. Even in this broken and fallen world, full of sin and decay, He is still in charge, He is still sovereign, and He still has all authority.

While we could go to countless passages to see this principle supported, for the sake of brevity, and because there shouldn't be any dispute at this point, we'll stick to one Old Testament and one New Testament book.

## IN THE BOOK OF DANIEL

In Daniel 2, when God revealed to Daniel the dream of Nebuchadnezzar and its meaning, Daniel gave thanks to God because "wisdom and might belong to Him. And He changes the times and the seasons; He removes kings and establishes kings;" (Daniel 2:20b-21a). Daniel recognized the authority of God - the ultimate authority over rulers and kings, and even times and seasons.

Then in chapter 4, after Nebuchadnezzar has another dream that Daniel interprets for him, Daniel says, "this is the interpretation, O king, and this is the resolution of the Most High, which has reached my lord the king: that you be driven away from mankind, and your place of habitation be with the beasts of the field, and you be given grass to eat like cattle and be drenched with the dew of heaven; and seven periods of time will pass over you until you know that the Most High is the powerful ruler over the kingdom of mankind and gives it to whomever He wishes." (Daniel 4:24-25)

Daniel tells the most powerful earthly king the earth

had ever seen that there is another heavenly king, "the Most High," that will humble him and make him like a beast until he learns who is the most powerful king - that He rules over mankind, that all authority is His, and that he appoints whom He chooses.

After that prophecy has been fulfilled, Nebuchadnezzar comes to his senses and acknowledges that "His dominion is an everlasting dominion, and His kingdom endures from generation to generation. And all the inhabitants of the earth are accounted as nothing, but He does according to His will in the host of heaven and among the inhabitants of earth; and no one can strike against His hand or say to Him, 'What have You done?'" (Dan 4:34b-35)

The powerful earthly king was humbled and acknowledged the authority of the Most High. He was taught who the real boss was! He has all authority and does as He wishes; he has a kingdom that is eternal, He is sovereign over the unseen realm and over the earth, and nobody has the right to challenge His authority.

## In the Gospel of Mark

Having established from the Old Testament (and the conclusions from Daniel are echoed throughout it) that Yahweh, the God of Israel, has all authority, in the New Testament, we see the same is said of Christ. This is one of the many ways that the New Testament communicates the deity of Christ. [1]

In Mark 1, Jesus teaches with authority (v22), and His deeds show his authority too (v27). When he later calms the storm, the disciples respond by asking each other in fear and astonishment, "Who then is this, that even the wind and the sea obey Him?" (Mark 4:41). In the Old Testament, Yahweh alone had authority over the elements - here Jesus is again shown to be God as He has authority not just over the demonic realm and people, but over the wind and waves too.

This same theme of authority is seen throughout Mark's gospel - from the obvious and numerous miracles to the taking of a colt with a mere "the Lord has need of it" (Mark 11:3) and the cursing of the fig tree (Mark 11:12-14).

## THE SUPREME CHRIST

The authority of God can be seen throughout both the Old and New Testaments. In the Old Testament, Yahweh is declared to be the creator and sovereign over all; in the New Testament, Jesus Christ, Yahweh incarnate, is equally declared to be the creator and sovereign over all. Christ is supreme over all - creator,

1  See "Putting Jesus in His Place: The Case for the Deity of Christ" by Rob Bowman and Ed Komoszewski (Kregel, 2007) for the HANDS acronym. Jesus has the Honor, the Attributes, the Names, does the same Deeds and sits in the same Seat (authority) as the Father. Each is evidence of His deity.

sustainer, and ruler.

In Philippians 2, Paul reminds us that what was said of Yahweh in Isaiah 45 will ultimately be fulfilled in Christ; that one day every knee will bow, and every tongue will confess Him as Lord and God - in Heaven, on earth, and under the earth - to the glory of God the Father. All authority is His, and one day we will all see that and acknowledge it and give account to Him alone.

These brief examples from Daniel, Mark, and Philippians will suffice for now as we move on to our next foundational principle. Still, everything moving forward from here is built upon this primary foundation - that all authority is God's. All of it. Every last bit. If there is any authority in all of creation, it is ultimately His.

*"And He went up on the mountain and summoned those whom He Himself wanted, and they came to Him. And He appointed twelve (whom He also named apostles) to be with Him and to send them out to preach and to have authority to cast out the demons."* MARK 3:13-15

# 2

## GOD DELEGATES HIS AUTHORITY AS HE CHOOSES, BUT IT REMAINS HIS

Our second foundational principle is that God, who has all authority, can and does delegate that authority to others, but when He does so, that authority remains His. He does not give it away. It does not change ownership. He does not divest Himself of authority. It is still His, but somebody has been delegated to exercise a portion of His authority on His behalf.

A clear example of this is seen when Jesus sends out His disciples. His authority is shown as He calls those He wants, and they come (Mark 3:13). Having called them, he sends them out with authority to cast out demons as He Himself had done (Mark 6:7). They were not allowed or able to cast out demons beforehand - there was nothing in themselves that gave them either the authority or the ability to do so. Note that

Judas was amongst them, and he was not even saved! So neither the might nor the authority was granted on the basis of faith even - it was simply what Jesus chose to do. They were granted both the permission and the power to do so by the One who has all might and authority (Jude 25). They had that role, not because of any authority of their own, but because it was delegated to them by the One who had it all.

Another example of delegated authority comes to us from Isaiah 10, where God uses Assyria to punish Israel's sin and idolatry. He describes Assyria as "the rod of My anger and the staff in whose hands is My indignation" (Isa 10:5). In other words, God, who has authority to punish Israel chooses to do so through delegated authority - through an unbelieving Gentile nation even! So it seems that the delegating of authority to Judas was not without precedent. In fact, many times in the Old Testament, God uses foreign nations to discipline and judge Israel. Nebuchadnezzar, long before his humbling and acknowledging of God's authority, is called God's servant and delegated authority to invade and destroy Jerusalem (Jeremiah 25:9).

In Scripture, the delegation of God's authority begins as early as Genesis 1:28, where man is given dominion over the earth. The earth does not become man's in the sense that man can say to God, "I'm in charge and will do as I will"; the earth remains God's. He made it, and He has all authority over it. But He delegated some of His authority to man. Man gets dominion over the earth, not instead of God, but on behalf of God.

## DELEGATED AUTHORITY REMAINS HIS

A simple analogy of this type of delegation is renting a car. When you rent a car, you drive it, but if you are in an accident, you are responsible for it. Why? Because it is not your car - you simply had the use of it. It would be your responsibility to repair any damage and return the car in the same condition as you were given it. So it is with delegated authority: it remains God's authority even if and when it is delegated to us. We are responsible for the rightful and obedient use of that delegated authority.

Before we move on to the next principle, let us consider the implications of this for us in life in general. I am a husband and a father - I have been delegated authority in my home. I am a pastor and have delegated authority in the church. But these are delegated authorities and not my own. I am exercising God's authority as His servant, and I am accountable for that. Such delegated authority should not lead to arrogance, self-importance, or a tyrannical reign, but rather should result in fear and humility, constantly aware of whom I am representing. This should have been true for Judas, Assyria, and Nebuchadnezzar - it should be true for secular leaders as much as for believers, though it is rarely the case in practice.

"But when he became strong, his heart was so proud that he acted corruptly, and he was unfaithful to Yahweh his God. And he entered the temple of Yahweh to burn incense on the altar of incense.

Then Azariah the priest entered after him and with him eighty priests of Yahweh, men of valor. And they stood against Uzziah the king and said to him, "It is not for you, Uzziah, to burn incense to Yahweh, but for the priests, the sons of Aaron who are set apart as holy to burn incense. Get out of the sanctuary, for you have been unfaithful and will have no honor from Yahweh God."

But Uzziah, with a censer in his hand for burning incense, was enraged; and while he was enraged with the priests, the leprosy broke out on his forehead before the priests in the house of Yahweh, beside the altar of incense.

And Azariah the chief priest and all the priests looked at him, and behold, he was leprous on his forehead; and they hurried him out of there, and he himself also hastened to get out because Yahweh had smitten him.

So King Uzziah was a leper to the day of his death; and he lived in a separate house, being a leper, for he was cut off from the house of Yahweh. And Jotham his son was over the king's house, judging the people of the land." 2 Chronicles 26:16-21

# 3

## ALL DELEGATED AUTHORITY IS LIMITED IN PERSON

When authority is delegated by God, it is always limited. Every single time without exception. God never gives His authority over all of Heaven and earth to any other. Thus all delegated authority is limited. And it is limited in three different ways - limited in person, limited in realm or sphere, and limited in extent. When authority is delegated, it is to a specific person or people to do specific work and within specific parameters.

With the rental car analogy, if you rent a car, you cannot let just anybody drive it - they have to be named and of a certain age. The authority to drive the car is limited in person. You are renting the car to drive on the road - you would not be permitted to drive through rivers, to use it for maintenance practice, or any other purpose. The authority to use the car is limited in realm or sphere - it has a specific limited purpose. And the rental company may put limits on mileage per day and on other practicalities such as crossing borders and driving in other countries. So even while using the vehicle in the right sphere, there may be limitations on the extent of the authority to use the car. And as the renter, you don't get to determine those limitations - it's not your car. The limitations are determined by the rental company that owns the vehicle.

We see the same in Genesis 1. God delegates authority of dominion. That delegated authority is limited in person - mankind is given that authority, not the angelic realm. That authority is also limited in realm - it is over the earth and the things in the earth, not the heavenly realm. And finally, even when the delegated person is operating in the delegated realm, there are limitations to the extent of that authority - they are not permitted to eat meat at this point (despite having authority over animals, the authority to kill and eat them is not given until the Noahic covenant) but can eat fruit from all the trees, except from the tree of knowledge of good and evil (Genesis 2:17).

For the remainder of this chapter, we'll consider limitations in person.

## LIMITED IN PERSON

People inherently know that authority is limited in

person. For example, a parent with young children has authority over them - they get to tell them, broadly speaking, what they can and can't do. But suppose that parent goes into somebody else's home and starts telling other people's children what to do. In that case, they have no authority to do so - the authority of a parent over children is limited to their own children. The God-delegated authority over the children is limited to their parents, not merely any adult.

This is why the modern humanistic notion of children being the responsibility of the entire community is tyrannical and nefarious - the authority over those children is God's alone, and He has delegated it to parents (Eph 6:1). In the same way, God delegates authority in the home to the husband, but that does not give him authority over women in a general sense, but only over his own wife. Authority is always limited in person.

Imagine you are driving along, perhaps a little too fast, and you hear sirens from behind you. You look in your mirror and see the blue flashing lights. You pull over, kicking yourself for driving too fast, and await the inevitable ticket. Then out of the police car comes Greta Thunberg! She walks up to your window, looks you in the eye, scowls, and screams, "How dare you?!?" At this point, you know you are free to drive away ticketless. This Swedish child environmental campaigner has no authority to give you a ticket even if you were speeding, no matter how much she claims you stole her childhood!

It's a silly illustration, but it makes the point clearly: no matter how important somebody thinks they are, no matter how right they think they are, or how wrong they are sure you are, that doesn't give them authority. Neither Greta nor another disgruntled driver can follow you home and give you a ticket for speeding - they have no authority.

So if a person hasn't been delegated authority, they have no authority. And the only person who can ultimately delegate authority is God. Why? Because all authority is His.

## THE KING WHO WANTED TO BE A PRIEST AS WELL

A classic example of authority being limited in person that we find in Scripture is found in 2 Chronicles 26:16-21. King Uzziah of Judah, like Nebuchadnezzar after him, grew powerful - and his power led him to be proud (v16). And in his pride, he tried to take authority that was not delegated to him. That is how we often learn about authority in the Bible - when those who don't have it try and take it.

He enters the temple to burn incense (v16). This is a job that God has delegated to the priesthood. The priests were all from the tribe of Levi under the Old Covenant; the kings were from the tribe of Judah. Different tribes were delegated with authority for different roles. The high priest knew the seriousness of Uzziah's boundary-breaking here and chased after him with 80 other priests - men of valor, thus presumably physically strong or courageous (v17). They stood up to the king. This, at first glance, might seem like a brazen thing to do - the king was surely in charge, was he not? Could he not have killed them for them standing up to him? But the priests understood the limitations of delegated authority. "They stood against Uzziah the king and said to him, 'It is not for you, Uzziah, to burn incense to Yahweh, but for the priests, the sons of Aaron who are set apart as holy to burn incense. Get out of the sanctuary, for you have been unfaithful and will have no honor from Yahweh God.'" (v18)

The priests took a huge personal risk in standing up against the king. They, not the king, had been delegated priestly authority; in his pride, he had decided that their authority was under his rule. Their bravery in standing up to him showed that they feared God, who delegated authority to them and to whom they were accountable, more than they feared man, even though that man was king. In this biblical precedent, obedience to God required defiance to the king.

Uzziah, who already had the censer for the incense in his hand, reacts to them with great anger, but God immediately intervenes and strikes Uzziah with leprosy (v19). His leprosy meant that he who sought to take authority over the house of God was unable to enter it again as he remained a leper until his death (vv.20-21). He did not heed the priests' cry to "get out of the sanctuary!" so God removed him permanently. The authority of the priestly duties was allocated to the sons of Aaron, from the tribe of Levi, not to the king. Scripture is clear: authority is limited in person.

*"Then the king arose at dawn, at the break of day, and hurriedly went to the lions' den.*

*When he had come near the den to Daniel, he cried out with a troubled voice. The king answered and said to Daniel, "Daniel, servant of the living God, has your God, whom you constantly serve, been able to save you from the lions?"*

*Then Daniel spoke to the king, "O king, live forever!*

*My God sent His angel and shut the lions' mouths, and they have not harmed me, inasmuch as I was found innocent before Him; and also toward you, O king, I have done no harm."* DANIEL 6:19-22

# 4

## ALL DELEGATED AUTHORITY IS LIMITED IN REALM / SPHERE

Another way to look at the example of Uzziah is that while from one perspective, he was the wrong person, from another perspective, he was trying to exercise authority in the wrong realm or sphere. As king, he had authority, but his authority did not extend to the priestly realm. It didn't matter whether he liked that or not; as king he couldn't simply take that authority. Why? Because all authority is God's, and He delegates it to whom He chooses while it remains His. God delegates the authority of kingship and of the priesthood. The king cannot simply extend his realm because he is king. Delegated authority is limited in realm.

Note also how the text of 2 Chronicles specifically points out it was pride that led him to attempt to exercise authority outside his realm. Overreaching one's authority is almost always an issue of pride.

Another instructive biblical example of authority being limited in realm is found in the well-known story of Daniel in the lions' den (Daniel 6). King Darius (who likes Daniel) is tricked into making a decree saying that no petition is to be made to anyone, man or god, but the king for 30 days. Violation of this edict would result in being thrown into the lions' den. Under Me-do-Persian law, the law was above the king - the king could make a law, but then he was bound to it. He has to submit to the law he has made (vv.1-9).

The king had been given authority - it is God who raises up and removes kings, as we saw in Daniel 2. So he has the authority to make laws. But his authority does not extend to the realm of personal devotion - to whom one makes petitions and prayers.

And so, like the priests in the reign of Uzziah, Daniel responded with boldness to the tyrannical overreach of undelegated authority. Rather than hide away and pray quietly, maintaining his duty to God without personal risk, he opened his windows wide and boldly prayed so that all could see him (v.10). Not only did he not comply with the unauthorized mandate, but he openly and boldly showed that he was not submitting to it.

## UNJUST PUNISHMENT

So although the king had not been delegated the authority to make such a decree, he did it anyway. But this time, rather than striking the overreaching tyrant with leprosy, God allowed Daniel to be thrown into the lion's den. We'll deal with the issue of pragmatism later in the book, but we should note now that a king that does not have the authority to do something may still have the might and power to do it. At times God may intervene, and at other times he might not.

The intervention was immediate in the case of the priests and Uzziah; Daniel's intervention came after he was thrown into the lions' den. For others, whether it is Canadian pastors being imprisoned for holding church and rejecting the overreach of tyrannical leaders or whether the multitude of martyrs who have given their lives for the faith over the years, there is no intervention.

The ending of Daniel is well known - Darius regrets his decree and is delighted to hear Daniel has been rescued from the mouths of the lions by his God. What is often missed is that the reason Daniel gives for God's miraculous intervention is that he was innocent both before God and before the king (v.22). The significance of this must not be missed: though Daniel clearly and blatantly broke the decree of the king, he did nothing wrong, not only in the sight of God but even against the king who made it. Why? Because Darius had no authority to make that law. Right person; wrong realm. And in saying this, Daniel was ultimately seeking the King's best interest – speaking the truth and walking in love.

If a person to whom God has delegated authority steps into a realm beyond that which has been delegated to him, he has no authority there. It matters not whether that is, in his mind, a logical expansion, a justifiable expansion, or a requested expansion; if it has not been given to him by God, it is not his realm. Thus God's delegated authority is limited not only in person but also in realm.

"Now it happened in the morning that David wrote a letter to Joab and sent it by the hand of Uriah. And he had written in the letter, saying, "Place Uriah in the front line of the fiercest battle and withdraw from him, so that he may be struck down and die." So it was as Joab kept watch on the city, that he put Uriah at the place where he knew there were valiant men.

And the men of the city went out and fought against Joab, and some of the people among David's servants fell; and Uriah the Hittite also died."
2 SAM 11:14-17

# 5

## ALL DELEGATED AUTHORITY IS LIMITED IN EXTENT

Just as the overreach of Uzziah can be viewed as one of person or realm (depending on perspective), so also the overreach of Darius can be viewed as one of realm or extent. There is certainly a large degree of crossover in these helpful but artificial categories. The broader point remains true, though - all delegated authority is limited. In one sense, all limitations are limitations of extent.

We previously saw that God delegated authority to Assyria in Isaiah 10 - they were God's servant and agent of His wrath against Israel (v5). Yet a few verses later, God says, "I will punish the fruit of the arrogant heart of the king of Assyria and the pomp of his eyes which are raised high. For he has said, 'by the power of my hand and by my wisdom I did this" (v12-13a).

Assyria had the authority to judge Israel as God's servant, but in his heart, the king went beyond the limits of his delegated authority. His duty was as God's servant, not to declare himself to be god-like. His arrogance led him, like the other kings we have seen, to go beyond the limits of his delegated authority. He was the right person operating in the right realm, but he went further than he was entitled to go.

Similarly, in 2 Samuel 11, in the well-known story of David and Bathsheba, David saw her, slept with her, and impregnated her. This infidelity was also, as it always is, an overstepping of David's delegated realm. Bathsheba was not his wife. He had no business gazing upon her, seeking after her, and certainly not sleeping with her. She was outside his realm; she was in the realm of another.

In trying to cover his sinful tracks, David then tried to get Uriah to sleep with his wife so that it would be presumed the child was his. After this failed, David resorted to killing him. The plan was to send him into war, pull the troops back, leaving Uriah to die (v15). Joab, failing to intervene and hinder this injustice, executed David's command by dispatching Uriah in this way. In addition, many other men also died as collateral damage in the outworking of David's plot (v.17).

Did David have authority over battles, war, troops, and commands? Did he have the authority to order Joab to direct the troops in the way he chose? Yes! Joab was the delegated person, and this was part of David's delegated realm. He could tell troops to go into battle and to retreat, to move forwards and to move backward. But in seeking to use the war to resolve the ramifications of his infidelity, he went beyond the extent of his authority. He was God's servant, not a tyrant - he could not use his delegated authority for his own personal gain. He attempted to resolve his overreach into Uriah's home with another overreach on the battlefield.

The principle here is a crucial one to grasp. Just because one has been delegated authority in a particular realm does not give one liberty to do whatever one wants within that realm without limit. In particular, any ruler is a servant of God who is operating under His authority (even the unbelievers like Judas and Nebuchadnezzar) - because the authority is not his own, a ruler cannot use it for his own benefit, glory, and pleasure. Pride and authority always combine to lead one to err from God's limitations and move into the realm of tyranny.

## CONCLUSION OF FOUNDATIONAL PRINCIPLES

Although our survey has been brief, it is clear from Scripture that all authority is God's. It does not belong inherently to anybody else. But God has delegated some authority to others, though it always remains His. And all delegated authority is limited in person, realm, and extent.

So when we look at various human authorities, we are looking at God's servants, whether they are believers or unbelievers, whether they are aware of it or not. Their authority is delegated to them by God, and they have no authority other than that which He has delegated to them. Thus they are accountable to Him for how they wield that authority, in particular any breaches of the limitations of authority that He has delegated.

The key question facing any human authority which seeks to issue decrees of any kind is not, "Is this beneficial?" - it's rather, "What authority has God given?" In the same way, the key question for those of us under such authority is not only, "Does this decree lead me to sin?" - it's rather, "Has God delegated such authority to this leader?"

Because aside from any God-delegated authority, they have none at all.

*"The Magistrate is an ordinance of God for the honor to good works, and a terror to evil works (Romans 13). Therefore when he begins to be a terror to good works and honor to evil, there is no longer in him, because he does thus, the ordinance of God, but the ordinance of the devil. And he who resists such works, does not resist the ordinance of God, but the ordinance of the devil."*

The Magdeburg Confession, 1550

*"There are limits prescribed by God to their [kings'] power, within which they ought to be satisfied: namely, to work for the common good and to govern and direct the people in truest fairness and justice; not to be puffed up with their own importance, but to remember that they also are subjects of God."*

JOHN CALVIN, *Sermon on 1 Samuel 8*, 16th Century

*"The civil sword cannot act either in restraining the souls of the people from worship or in constraining them to worship."*

ROGER WILLIAMS, *The Hireling Ministry None of Christ*, 1652

*"God has ordained the state as a delegated authority; it is not autonomous. The state is to be an agent of justice, to restrain evil by punishing the wrongdoer and to protect the good in society. When it does the reverse, it has no proper authority. It is then a usurped authority and as such it becomes lawless and is tyranny."*

FRANCIS SCHAEFFER, *A Christian Manifesto*, 1982

# Part Two

## WHAT HAS CAESAR BEEN DELEGATED?

"Then the Pharisees went and took counsel together about how they might trap Him in what He said.

And they sent their disciples to Him, along with the Herodians, saying, "Teacher, we know that You are truthful and teach the way of God in truth, and defer to no one; for You are not partial to any.

Therefore, tell us, what do You think? Is it lawful to give a tax to Caesar, or not?"

But Jesus, knowing their wickedness, said, "Why are you testing Me, you hypocrites?

Show Me the coin used for the tax." And they brought Him a denarius.

And He said to them, "Whose likeness and inscription is this?"

They said to Him, "Caesar's." Then He said to them, "Therefore, render to Caesar the things that are Caesar's; and to God the things that are God's."

And hearing this, they marveled, and leaving Him, they went away." MATTHEW 22:15-22

# 6

## CAESAR DOES NOT DECIDE WHAT IS HIS

Having laid down the key foundational biblical principles of authority, we are now equipped to look at the specific issue of Caesar - civil government.

We know that all authority belongs to God. So any authority that Caesar has, he has because God has given it to him. It doesn't matter if he is a believer or not, or whether he acknowledges God or not. Every Caesar, major or minor, every person on the ladder of human government with authority over others, is a servant of God - delegated authority by Him and for Him.

It is clear from Scripture that Caesar has been delegated authority. We can find the principles of human government as far back as the Noahic covenant in Gen 9, though it is beyond the scope of this present work to trace that through biblical history. Suffice it to say, we have already seen in Daniel 2 that God is the one who appoints kings and removes kings, he lifts them up and humbles them, and He has clearly given them a realm of some sort.

In Matthew 22:21, we have the well-known expression "Render to Caesar the things that are Caesar's; and to God the things that are God's." At the bare minimum, this tells us that there are things that belong to Caesar - that he has a realm. But importantly, we must not isolate this expression and think that Caesar's realm is no longer part of God's authority, for we know that all authority belongs to God. Yet there is clearly a realm that has been delegated to Caesar. And it is equally clear that there are things that God has not delegated to him.

So the question now is not only, as the majority of Christians seemingly believe, "is what I am being ordered to do sinful or not?" The question is also this: "what authority has God delegated to Caesar?" We will look at that shortly when we come to examine Romans 13, but for now, we should note something that must underpin that examination - Caesar has no authority apart from that which God has granted him.

To come at it from a different perspective, we must render to Caesar the things that are his, but Caesar does not get to decide what those things are. Only God does. Because all authority belongs to Him.

This is a revolutionary concept for many today. Yet

it is inescapably biblical. The reason that it seems so radical to us is that we have become so imperceptibly accustomed to the worldview of statism.

## STATISM—THE GOVERNMENT AS GOD

The Bible, as we have seen, teaches that all authority is God's, so any authority that Caesar possesses has been delegated to him by God. Thus he is accountable to God for his exercising of that delegated authority. The limits of that delegated authority are defined by God and not by Caesar. But when Caesar removes God from the equation, who then decides the limits of Caesar's authority? Of course, it will be Caesar! And in doing so, Caesar, whether he is aware of it or not, is taking the place of God - he is making himself a god. G.K. Chesterton famously said that "Once abolish the God, and the Government becomes the God."[1] This is statism.

Humanity was created to be image-bearers of our creator. We have an innate need for God - we are hard-wired to worship, and so we will, whether it is God or not. Our sinful nature means we want to reject Him and His commands, but nonetheless, our hearts naturally incline to worship of some sort. So when Caesar removes God from his thinking, he tends to make himself a replacement god.

Statism has become the norm today. We are now so readily accustomed to it that most of us, Christians

1 "Christendom in Dublin", G.K. Chesterton, 1932

included, accept it without question. Even in America, a country that was founded in a manner specifically to resist the inevitable encroachment of statism, such a worldview has taken hold.

"Can Caesar make that decree?" "Sure he can!" "Why?" "Because he's Caesar!" Statism is the worldview that Caesar is no longer a servant of God; rather, he has effectively been made into a god - he has, to some degree, taken over the role of God in our lives.

It is no use for us to plead that we do not worship Caesar because we worship Christ. Did not the Israelites in the Old Testament worship Yahweh while at the same time committing idolatry? Caesar rarely, if ever, desires to be a monotheistic god - he is happy to be worshipped alongside others. The issue was not so much that they had completely disowned Yahweh, but rather that they had viewed Him to be insufficient and had added other gods in certain realms. They might still observe the day of atonement, but that didn't stop them from making an offering to Baal for a better harvest.

Caesar has been delegated authority by the only one who can - God. But when he rejects the one who delegates authority to him, he now creates his own boundaries, or lack thereof, in lieu of God. He is the one who now delegates authority; he is now the one who determines his purpose and his limits; he is now the rule maker, the king, the ruler, the one to be feared and obeyed. Caesar has declared himself a god.

Let me be abundantly clear on this point. If we, as Christians, accept and embrace Caesar's self-declaration of deity, either by his explicit declaration or by his practical behavior, we are idolaters. We must give serious thought to how it is any different from the Yahweh worshippers who also sacrificed to Baal when we who profess Christ also bow before Caesar as he takes authority that God never gives him. No doubt, there are times when we can ignore his false authority with little consequence and times when we can perhaps reconcile some rulings as being part of some sort of mutually agreed upon social contract. But a line must be drawn nonetheless.

If a president, prime minister, or governor decided tomorrow that we must all hop on one leg while in grocery stores on Fridays, I hope that at this point in our journey, we would respond with a chuckle and a firm "no." We know that Caesar cannot simply do whatever he wants, and we would (rightly) presume that such nonsense is outside of his remit. Sadly, it has become clear that many in our society would do so. Even more sadly, many Christians would do so too, with cries of "Romans 13!" Statism has so corrupted our thinking that we can even twist Scripture to support it. Idolatry has always led to bad exegesis.

So we must go to Romans 13 and see what it says about the limitations of the authority that God has delegated to it. But first, we have one more stop to make - the church of Christ.

*"Obey your leaders and submit to them—for they keep watch over your souls as those who will give an account—so that they will do this with joy and not with groaning, for this would be unprofitable for you."* HEBREWS 13:17

*"Be on guard for yourselves and for all the flock, among which the Holy Spirit has made you overseers, to shepherd the church of God which He purchased with His own blood. I know that after my departure savage wolves will come in among you, not sparing the flock; and from among your own selves men will arise, speaking perverse things, to draw away the disciples after them. Therefore be watchful"* ACTS 20:28-31b

# 7

## The Church Is not Under Caesar's Rule

Ihave often joked that those who interpret Romans 13 as meaning that we should do whatever Caesar tells us to unless it is sinful should be consistent and take the same view of Hebrews 13:17. Then they'd be most welcome at our church. They'd presumably do whatever I tell them to do unless it were sinful!

It's funny how we can instinctively see the limitations of delegated authority more easily in the church than in government. Such is the impact of the slow but ever-greater incursions of statism.

That said, it is clear in that verse that authority in the church has not been delegated to Caesar. Pastors and elders have been delegated authority, with the practical assistance of deacons, to oversee the church (1 Tim 3, Titus 1, et al.). They have that authority and the huge responsibility that comes with it.

Paul's farewell to the Ephesian elders at Miletus in Acts 20 is particularly insightful. He warns the elders of those who will come in and try and harm the flock. Who does Paul say has the God-given role of defending and protecting the flock? Who is responsible for the sheep? Who has authority over them? Christ's under-shepherds! They have the authority and the burden of responsibility that comes with that.

Caesar has a domain, but his domain does not include the church. Kings and other various rulers have been given a domain, but the domain of the church was given to others - pastors and elders. God has appointed them, and no mere man can come along and say, "I'll have that, please!"

Do we think that the government cares more for our flocks? Do they understand at all, let alone consider, the spiritual well-being of the congregation? Do they know why we are told not to neglect meeting together (Heb 10:25)? Do they wrestle with the purpose and function of the church and how various decrees might hinder that work? Do they acknowledge the huge importance of the work of ministry at the gathering of the saints, or its ultimate conclusion: our conformity to Jesus Christ (Eph 4:11-16)? Can they comprehend that there are worse things than being physically sick or even dying?

## HANDING AUTHORITY OVER

When pastors who have been given the authority of the church hand it over to Caesar because Caesar, who wasn't given that authority, demands it, then they are accepting statism. Christ has entrusted His bride to them. When they then do to her everything Caesar, who rejects Christ's authority, demands that they do - what do we think Christ makes of this?

Those who hand over their delegated authority will be held accountable by Christ for bowing to Caesar's demands far more than others within the church. It is no small thing to hand over the reins to one who has rejected God when it is God who has chosen the church leaders to be His servants, God who has delegated them authority, and God who will hold them accountable for how the Church is overseen. It is akin to mutiny to be involved in overthrowing the leaders to whom God has delegated authority, even if you are those leaders!

This is no minor issue. Consider when Aaron and Miriam questioned the authority of Moses in Numbers 12 - it ends with God saying, "Why then were you not afraid to speak against My servant, against Moses?" (v8b), His anger burning (v9), and Miriam being struck with leprosy (v10). Or consider the rebellion of Korah and his accomplices in Numbers 16 - they assembled against Moses and Aaron, questioning their authority and pleading for equity, but ended up being swallowed by the ground, consumed by fire, and dying by plague. The usurping of God's delegated authority is a serious issue - it is ultimately a rebellion against God.

In the discussion of Romans 13, the rejection of God's authority is usually raised as an accusation against those who would not submit to Caesar's demands. But as we can see, it is perhaps just as appropriate to raise the issue of the rejection of God's authority to Caesar himself. When he tries to take authority that was not given to him, in particular the authority given to another, even more, so authority given over the bride of Christ, then it is he that needs to be warned. Historically this was often done by pastors and churches, yet with the encroaching of statism, the pulpits seem to have gone silent. Has the fear of Caesar overtaken the fear of God? Have we lost the spirit of boldness that the priests of Uzziah had?

Church leaders who have succumbed to the gradual encroachment of statism, whether intentionally or otherwise, have handed their God-delegated authority over to Caesar and allowed him to determine the parameters of the functioning of the local church.

The responsibility of a pastor is immense - he will be held to account for the shepherding of souls. And it is to him that this has been given, not Caesar. This mutinous dereliction of duty is tantamount to idolatry, even if one is blissfully unaware. We have one Lord and God to whom belongs all authority. One of my greatest desires for this little book is that it might call some leaders who have behaved in such a manner to repentance.

We who lead, in whatever realms, must all be more diligent in the exercise of our delegated authority. Tyranny is not limited to government - it is found in churches and homes too. I, for one, can look back on my life as a husband, father, and pastor and realize that I did not understand the ramifications of God's delegated authority as well as I should - the responsibility, the required servant-like humility, and the limitations. The responsibility of leaders not to overreach is rarely emphasized as much as the need for submission to those leaders.

*"Let love be without hypocrisy—by abhorring what is evil, clinging to what is good, being devoted to one another in brotherly love, giving preference to one another in honor, not lagging behind in diligence, being fervent in spirit, serving the Lord, rejoicing in hope, persevering in affliction, being devoted to prayer, contributing to the needs of the saints, pursuing hospitality.*

*Bless those who persecute you; bless, and do not curse. Rejoice with those who rejoice; weep with those who weep, by being of the same mind toward one another, not being haughty in mind, but associating with the humble. Do not be wise in your own mind.*

*Never paying back evil for evil to anyone, respecting what is good in the sight of all men, if possible, so far as it depends on you, being at peace with all men, never taking your own revenge, beloved—instead leave room for the wrath of God. For it is written, "Vengeance is Mine, I will repay," says the Lord. "But if your enemy is hungry, feed him, and if he is thirsty, give him a drink; for in so doing you will heap burning coals on his head." Do not be overcome by evil, but overcome evil with good."* ROMANS 12:9-21

*"Woe to those who call evil good and good evil,*

*Who substitute darkness for light and light for darkness,*

*Who substitute bitter for sweet and sweet for bitter!"* ISAIAH 5:20

# 8

## PUNISHING EVIL IS NOT IN OUR PERSONAL DOMAIN (ROMANS 12)

For us to understand the key passage of Romans 13, we need to begin with the preceding context. As was said in the introduction, our tendency to take a verse in isolation often leads to an overly simplistic and frequently inaccurate interpretation of the text. This is particularly true for Romans 13, as we will see.

In the book of Romans, broadly speaking, the first 11 chapters deal with theology, and then, in chapter 12, Paul starts dealing with the practicalities of the Christian life. Sacrifice, not being conformed to the world, service (through the exercising of spiritual gifts), and love are key themes in the early verses.

In verse 9, Paul introduces us to the principles of good and evil that become a crucial part of the context for the remainder of this chapter and into chapter 13.

He tells us that our love must be genuine or without hypocrisy and then tells us how we ensure that it is - "abhorring what is evil, clinging to what is good." If we don't hate evil and cling to good, our love may not be genuine love. This verse has echoes of Isaiah 5:20 that warns those who "call evil good and good evil." If we declare something to be loving and yet, in doing so, have clung to evil and hated what is good, our love is hypocritical and not genuine.

Only God can tell us what is evil, and we must hate that which he declares to be evil; only God can tell us what is good, and we must cling to that which He declares to be good. If anybody other than God defines what is good and evil, then the sinfulness of man places us in grave danger of getting into an Isaiah 5:20 situation. We would place ourselves at risk of the "woe to those" applying to us if we seek to define good and evil outside of Scripture. And every time Caesar does this, He goes beyond the limits of the authority he has been delegated. This understanding of good and evil underpins the next chapter and a half.

## THE STRUCTURE OF V.17-21

Verses 10-13 continue to describe genuine love. Then in verse 14, there is a principle to "Bless those who persecute you" - this introduces the key contextual issue for the remainder of the chapter that leads into the crucial verses: 17-21.

The structure here is what is known as a chiasm. A chiasm is a literary device in which a sequence of parallel outer layers puts the focus on the center of the written structure. If we had a sequence of ABCDCBA, the mirrored outer layers (ABC and CBA) would bring our focus onto the center (D). It's as if the ideas build to a crescendo and then mirror their way back out.

A chiastic structure is a great way of communicating thoughts in a memorable and focused way. "When the going gets tough, the tough get going" (ABBA) is a good example - "going" is followed by "tough," then it is mirrored on the way out with the repetition of "tough" before returning to "going."

Let's look at it visually:

v17: Never paying back **evil** for **evil** to anyone, respecting what is **good** in the sight of all men

    v.18: If possible, so far as it depends on you, being at peace with all men,

        v.19a: Never taking your own **revenge**, beloved

        v.19b: Instead, leave room for the **wrath** of God.

        v.19c: For it is written, "**Vengeance** is Mine, I will repay," says the Lord.

    v.20: "But if your enemy is hungry, feed him, and if he is thirsty, give him a drink; for in so doing you will heap burning coals on his head."

v.21 Do not be overcome by **evil,** but overcome **evil**

with **good**.

A: Evil x2 / Good
 B: Treat people well
  C: Vengeance
   D: The Wrath of God
  C: Vengeance
 B: Treat people well
A: Evil x2 / Good

In the outer layers, we have a double reference to "evil" and also a reference to "good" - these are key terms in the context of this passage. Then in the next layer, there are references to treating people well - "being at peace with all men" (v18) and loving your enemy (v20). When we get towards the center in verse 19, we have a double reference to vengeance: "never taking revenge" and "Vengeance is mine."

## VENGEANCE AND THE WRATH OF GOD

Combined, these give a clear message - we are not to take revenge ourselves because vengeance belongs to God. Then sandwiched in the very center is "the wrath of God." The contextual links to God-defined good and evil in verse 9 are clear to see - when evil is done to us, we are not to take vengeance but respond with goodness.

As a whole, this passage is saying that when we are treated badly by our enemies, we do not have the right to respond to their evil with further evil - rather, we are to respond in love. But why is it that we instinctively desire to repay evil with evil? Of course, our sinful nature plays the larger part in that. But is there not also a desire for justice? Does righteousness not demand justice in the face of evil? There is in this passage an assurance of justice - we are not permitted to take revenge, but God will take vengeance in lieu of us. There will still be an outworking of His wrath. So we can rest in that and respond with love and good treatment in response, leaving justice in the hands of God.

So if a murderer kills your child, there must be justice for that evil. Righteousness demands that evil must be dealt with. But it is not your role to execute that judgment - you have not been delegated that authority. Though a great evil was done to you or your family, you do not automatically get, nor can you take, the authority to mete out justice. Who has that authority? God does. Why? Because all authority is His.

## GOD-DEFINED GOOD AND EVIL

As we said regarding verse 9, He is also the only one who gets to define what is good and evil. When God created the heavens and the earth, He declared His work to be good (Gen 1) - he made it, it was His, and it was good. So when we are told to "overcome evil with good" (v21), it is God who declares what qualifies as an evil that must be overcome and what qualifies as the good that must overcome it. When we are told not to "repay evil for evil," it is God that determines what is evil and when we are told to "respect what is good in the sight of all men" (v17), He determines what is good.

It is not those in whose sight we are to do that good who get to decide (as it might seem at first glance) - often, people call good what God calls evil and vice versa (Isa 5:20). The broader context clarifies that Paul is not speaking of us doing what they define as good, but what God defines as good so that they might see it. In the same way, nor does Caesar get to determine what is good - he cannot simply say "this is for your good" and be justified in his declaration. Any decree of Caesar must be within the limitations of the authority that has been delegated to him - and part of those limitations is God's biblical definitions of what is good and what is evil.

Now, after building a foundation of broad biblical principles and establishing the immediately preceding context, we can finally take a close look at our key passage - Romans 13.

"*Every person is to be in subjection to the governing authorities. For there is no authority except from God, and those which exist have been appointed by God. Therefore whoever resists that authority has opposed the ordinance of God; and they who have opposed will receive condemnation upon themselves. For rulers are not a cause of fear for good behavior, but for evil. Do you want to have no fear of that authority? Do what is good, and you will have praise from the same; for it is a minister of God to you for good. But if you do what is evil, be afraid; for it does not bear the sword in vain, for it is a minister of God, an avenger who brings wrath on the one who practices evil. Therefore it is necessary to be in subjection, not only because of that wrath, but also because of conscience.*" ROMANS 13:1-5

# 9

## PUNISHING EVIL HAS BEEN DELEGATED TO CAESAR (ROMANS 13)

Most modern Bible-believing Christians, who are so used to dealing with verses in isolation from their context, read Romans 13:1a, that "every person is to be in subjection to the governing authorities" and presume that this half of a verse settles all discussion. "See! You have to submit to Caesar!" And yet that verse does not even mention government.

"Governing" authorities means "higher" or "superior" authorities. The statement is a general principle: submit to those who have been delegated authority over you. At this point, it tells us nothing of who those authorities are or what authority has been delegated to them. Paul states the general principle before going on to the specifics.

This passage is not alone in its adoption of such

a structure. In Ephesians 5:20, Paul lists various out-workings of being filled in the Spirit, the last of which is "being subject to one another in the fear of Christ." There is no mention in that verse of who to submit to, just that submission flows out of a Spirit-filled life. Then in verse 21, a specific example is given: "wives be subject to your own husbands as unto the Lord"; then another in 6:1: "Children obey your parents," and another in 6:5: "Slaves, be obedient to those who are your masters according to the flesh." Peter adopts this same structure as well. In 1 Peter 2:13a, he starts with the general principle, "Be subject for the sake of the Lord to every human institution" before going on to give specifics: "whether to a king as the one in authority or to governors as sent by him" (v13b-14a).

Though Paul goes on to speak of civil government from verse 3, it remains a great irony that the half of a verse most quoted in the discussion on submission to Caesar doesn't even mention civil government! Hence the importance of understanding verses in their context and not in isolation.

## SUBMISSION FOR GOD; SUBMISSION TO GOD

So the general principle Paul begins with is to submit to the delegated authorities above you. Yes, it applies to submission to civil government (as will be clarified as Paul goes from the general to the specific), but it also applies to wives (to their husbands), children (to their parents), and slaves (to their masters). And it also applies to American law enforcement officers, judges, mayors, governors, and presidents submitting to the United States constitution, and, far more importantly, to all rulers in and of all nations submitting to the God from whom their delegated authority is derived. Everyone, everywhere, in every time, must submit to God.

The reason why such submission must occur is spelled out very clearly in the second half of verse 1: "For there is no authority except from God, and those which exist have been appointed by God." This is one of the clearest verses in Scripture on our second principle - that of delegated authority. The reason, the only reason, why we submit to other humans is because God, who has all authority, tells us to. In submitting to them, we are, in fact, submitting to Him because He tells us to do so.

When one understands that Romans 13 must constantly be viewed from another angle - Caesar must be submitted to within the limits of his delegated authority, but Caesar must also submit, without limit, to the God who has all authority.

Thus Romans 13:1 should not be wielded at Christians by tyrannical leaders as if the matter of obedience to their every whim is settled. Rather it should strike fear into the heart of every leader - of every husband, of every parent, of every pastor, and of every ruler at whatever level of human government. All to whom

God has delegated authority are accountable to Him. All leaders, in any realm of life, should be sobered by this truth and should do all they can, in fearful reverence to God, to avoid ever straying beyond the limits and purposes of the authority that has been delegated to them.

Thus when we consider verse 2 and its warning not to resist, it should be perceived as a warning not only to those under the leadership of another but also to the leaders themselves. The general principle of submission is for all people to submit to higher authorities that have been delegated by God, and if they don't, they will become subject to condemnation. As much as this general principle and its warning of judgment would apply to a citizen breaking a biblically valid law, a rebellious wife, or a disobedient young child, it would also apply to an American judge who disregards the Constitution's authorial intent, a British mayor that places illegal restrictions on protests, a third world dictator who does as he wishes with no thought of God, a law enforcement officer who imposes ungodly or unauthorized restrictions, a husband who seeks to control his wife, and a president who calls good evil, and evil good.

## THE ROLE OF CAESAR

When we come to the "rulers" in verses 3-5, the general principle of submission is now specifically applied.

At last, we get to the specifics of submission to Caesar.

The first thing to note here is the very deliberate connections between chapters 12 and 13. Keywords and concepts from chapter 12 are repeated in chapter 13, showing the connection between these two passages - "good," "evil," vengeance, and "wrath." Remember that the chapter break is not inspired, and these two passages naturally flow from one to the other.

"Good" and "evil," as we saw earlier, were mentioned in 12:9, then again in 12:17 and 21 (with evil used twice in both those later verses). At the center of the chiasm in v.17-21 was a double reference to vengeance ("revenge" in v19 and "vengeance" in v21), and right in the middle was the centerpiece: "the wrath of God."

This can be hard to see in some English versions. The ESV, for example, is particularly poor in its consistency. In chapter 12 of the ESV, we have "evil" (vv.9,17,21), then "bad" and "wrong" for the same Greek word in chapter 13 (vv.3,4), losing the connection between the two passages. I have therefore used the more consistent Legacy Standard Bible throughout this book. Be assured that the LSB's repetition of these words mirrors the repetition in the Greek text.

| ESV | LSB |
|---|---|
| "For rulers are not a terror to good conduct, but to bad" | "...but to evil" (v3) |

| ESV | LSB |
|---|---|
| "But if you do wrong, be afraid" | "But if you do what is evil" (v4a) |
| "Who carries out God's wrath on the wrongdoer" | "...on the evildoer" (v4b) |

So when we see in verse 3, "For rulers are not a cause of fear for good behavior, but for evil," we have a deliberate connection to the end of chapter 12. As we saw there, it is God who determines what is good and what is evil, and woe to those that redefine those words. So if someone does what is right in God's eyes, they should have nothing to fear from Caesar; conversely, those who do what God defines as evil should be in fear of the government.

More so, in addition to not living in fear of Caesar, those who do what God defines as good should be receiving praise from Caesar (v3b). The same is said in 1 Peter 2:14, which speaks of Caesar as being sent by God "for the punishment of evildoers and the praise for those who do good."

The reason given for this ideal scenario is clearly stated in verse 4 - "it is a minister of God to you for good." Caesar's authority is delegated authority granted to him by God for the purpose of ministering on behalf of God for good, as defined by God. Ministering for good is clearly not limited to praising those who do good; it is also good in God's eyes when evil is punished. "But if you do what is evil, be afraid; for it does not bear the sword in vain, for it is a minister of God, an avenger who brings wrath on the one who practices evil." Caesar ministers for good and for God - this involves rewarding those who do good and punishing those who do evil, which is why Caesar can legitimately wield the sword of punishment.

## GOD'S AVENGING SERVANT

In verse 4 alone, we see the use of the words "good," "evil," and "wrath," and the concept of vengeance ("avenger"). They connect what is being said here with the end of chapter 12. There we learned that it was not our responsibility to punish evil done to us - God has not delegated that authority to those who have been harmed. Ultimately He will have vengeance, not us because the wrath against that evil is rightly His and not ours. This has echoes of David's Psalm of repentance, where he declares, "Against You, and You only, have I sinned and done what's evil in Your sight. So that You are justified when You speak and pure when You judge." (Psalm 51:4). All sin is ultimately against God; He will execute vengeance and judgment - it is His wrath.

Now in 13:4, we see that God takes His vengeance and pours out His wrath by means of a delegated avenger. In chapter 12, we learned that punishing evil was God's duty, and He did not delegate it to the victims; in chapter 13, we learn that he has delegated it to Caesar. So the end of chapter 12 and the beginning of chapter 13 combine to tell us that the punishment of evil is not to be done by those who would feel the greatest need for justice - the victims and their loved ones - but rather by civil government, soberly judging the crime and handing down the sentence, as a servant of God seeking to uphold His justice on His behalf.

We can all, no doubt, see the wisdom in this. If any serious evil was done against one of my children, I would no doubt feel a degree of righteous anger - anger that would be shared in the heart of God. I am, however, not naive enough to pretend that my sinful anger would not only blend with any righteous anger but would completely overwhelm it. I would not be someone who could be trusted to act rationally and fairly. I could not be expected to separate myself from my emotions and personal loss sufficiently to make a sober judgment. God has made Caesar His servant to execute such sober judgment on behalf of the victims, society at large, and ultimately, Himself.

Paul then gives us two reasons to submit to Caesar - the punishment he can legitimately execute on behalf of God and our conscience in knowing we have done what God has called evil (v5).

So Caesar's limited, delegated authority has been defined: he is a minister of God, serving Him through His delegated authority, in the praising and rewarding

of what God defines as good and in the punishing of
what God defines as evil.

*"When a ruler uses his authority for purposes just the reverse of those for which it was delegated to him - when he evidently encroaches on the natural and constitutional rights of the subject - when he tramples on those laws which were made, at once to limit his power, and defend the people - in such cases they are not obliged to obey him. They are guilty of impiety against God; and of injustice to themselves, and the community of which they are members if they do."*
JASON HAVEN, *Congregationalist Minister*, 1769

*"When the civil authority trespasses the limits of its authority, it is the duty of the church to condemn such a violation."*
JOHN MURRAY, *Collected Writings*, 1950s

*"If there is no final place for civil disobedience, then the government has been made autonomous, and as such, it has been put in the place of the living God. ...And that point is exactly when the early Christians performed their acts of civil disobedience, even when it cost them their lives. ...Acts of State which contradict God's Law are illegitimate and acts of tyranny. Tyranny is ruling without the sanction of God. To resist tyranny is to honour God. ...The bottom line is that at a certain point there is not only the right, but the duty to disobey the State.[12]"*
FRANCIS SCHAEFFER, *A Christian Manifesto*, 1983

*"If the state becomes a terror to those who do good and rewards those who do evil, it is again in flagrant violation of God's command and ordinance, and Christians have at that point a duty to resist an authority that has ceased to be God's deacon."*
JOSEPH BOOT, *For Politics: The Christian, The Church And The State*, 2021

# Part Three

## Responding to a Biblical Understanding of Authority

"So then, my beloved, just as you have always obeyed, not as in my presence only, but now much more in my absence, work out your salvation with fear and trembling; for it is God who is at work in you, both to will and to work for His good pleasure." PHILIPPIANS 2:12-13

"Therefore I, the prisoner in the Lord, exhort you to walk worthy of the calling with which you have been called, with all humility and gentleness, with patience, bearing with one another in love, being diligent to keep the unity of the Spirit in the bond of peace." EPHESIANS 4:1-3

# 10

## How Do We Respond?

What we have learned in this study so far should have enabled us to put aside statism (seemingly the default position in today's society, even amongst believers) and embrace a biblical understanding of the issues of authority, civil government, and specifically where they combine with the Church.

While this may well have answered many general questions such as how we should interpret Romans 13 and what the purpose of government is, it not only leaves many specific questions unanswered, it has probably increased them dramatically. The ramifications of what we have seen are huge!

We now know what the role of Caesar is - he is God's avenging servant, punishing evil and rewarding good. But what happens when, as is typically the case,

Caesar is evil? And what if he is not just a little bit evil, but what if he actually starts rewarding evil and punishing good? How do we respond to him then? If he is not acting as God's servant as God requires him to, can we dismiss him and his mandates completely?

If Caesar were to say (again) that we were forbidden to meet or to sing, then we know he has no God-delegated authority to do so. But what if you do continue to meet and there are consequences imposed by Caesar that he is not authorized to make? Church leaders today are being confronted with this harsh reality as they live with Caesars, who are threatening to punish them with severe consequences for doing things that God has called "good."

If only we could turn to the Bible and get clear, direct, and specific answers to every potential decision we have to make in light of Caesar's mandates! So many of the decisions we must make are neither right nor wrong biblically. It is not a sin to put a mask on our face, per se, nor to not wear one. But how should we respond when Caesar, going beyond his God-delegated authority, tells us we must? In church? In grocery stores? Knowing that he has no authority to make such mandates does not in and of itself resolve how we might respond to them.

And what about other issues that, when we were blinded by statism, used to be non-issues? Does Caesar have the authority to set speed limits? Surely driving at

100mph past a school in a 30mph limit as the children head home is evil, but what about driving at a 35mph limit at midnight? Coming to a biblical understanding of authority should make us rethink so much of what we had taken for granted - even if we end up at the same conclusions in practice.

If we hold that the Bible is not only authoritative but also sufficient (and we should), how do we navigate its silence on so many difficult decisions that need to be made when living under a tyrannical Caesar? How do we walk in a manner that is worthy of our calling (Eph 4:1) in such a hostile environment?

In the final part of this small book, I will be dealing with various considerations and implications arising from the first two parts. I need to once again remind the reader (and myself!) that I am not a doctor nor a lawyer - my only task here is to teach the Bible. So I will continue to try to avoid giving my opinion on the efficacy (or lack thereof) of "vaccines"[1] and masks or on any constitutional or legal issue in any particular country. The outworking of that will be that there are likely to be a whole bunch of gray areas where you may

1   The use of quotation marks around "vaccine" is not intended to be pejorative in any way, but simply to acknowledge that the way in which these "vaccines" work is definitely different from how vaccines work. The methodology is sufficiently different that using the same terminology is perhaps more misleading than not. To avoid wading into the debate I have opted simply to put the word in quotes to try to both annoy and pacify both sides in equal measures.

like to have definitive answers, but you may ultimately be left with more questions than you began with! But that's ok, as we shall see.

"Be subject for the sake of the Lord to every human institution, whether to a king as the one in authority, or to governors as sent by him for the punishment of evildoers and the praise of those who do good.

For such is the will of God that by doing good you may silence the ignorance of foolish men.

Act as free people, and do not use your freedom as a covering for evil, but use it as slaves of God.

Honor all people, love the brethren, fear God, honor the king...."

"For to this you have been called, since Christ also suffered for you, leaving you an example that you should follow in His steps, who did no sin, nor was any deceit found in His mouth; who being reviled, was not reviling in return; while suffering, He was uttering no threats, but kept entrusting Himself to Him who judges righteously." 1 PETER 2:13-17, 21-23

# 11

## EVIL CAESARS

One misunderstanding that often arises is around the issue of bad Caesars. What happens when Caesar is evil? We typically see two opposite views in this regard.

Firstly, there is the suggestion that if Caesar is evil, then we can disregard him altogether - "he is supposed to be God's servant!" This view allows us to dismiss Caesar and everything he says. Secondly, there is the belief that no matter how bad Caesar is, we must still submit. This was the view of many pastors in Germany under the Nazis during World War II.

The latter view can be swiftly dismissed on the basis of what we have learned thus far in our study of Scripture. We have already seen that submission to Caesar is dependent upon Caesar operating within the limited authority that God has delegated to him. But what about the other view? Do our conclusions thus far warrant a dismissal of all commands by a tyrannical Caesar?

1 Peter 2:13-17 is the key passage for this issue. It begins, as previously noted, with a general statement about submitting to those we are supposed to submit to (v13a) - "every human institution" includes families and churches as well as Caesar. The remainder of the verses, in isolation, tells us nothing more than we have seen already in our studies - rulers in civil government are sent by God "for the punishment of evildoers and the praise of those who do good" (v14),

## RIGHTEOUSNESS IN THE FACE OF EVIL

When seen only in isolation, these verses might be able to be used to support the idea of the complete rejection of an evil Caesar. Like in Romans 13, an idealistic scenario is portrayed - compare "for rulers are not a cause for fear for good behavior, but for evil" (Roms 13:3a) and "that by doing good, you may silence the ignorance of foolish men" (1 Peter 2:15b), for example.

Accounting for this idealism in the immediate context, and remembering the broader principles we have seen, might lead us to view "honor the king" in a similar idealistic way - we might understand it in the sense of "honor to whom honor is due" and determine that if Caesar is going beyond the limits that God has given him, then he is not worthy of such honor. In other words, we might be tempted to conclude that an evil Caesar, because he is not acting as a servant of God as he should be, is not worthy of either our honor or our obedience.

The broader context of this passage, however, does not allow us to make such a conclusion. This "household code,"[1] while similar to the ones we find in Ephesians and Colossians, has a unique twist - it emphasizes the importance of submitting even when the one we are submitting to is ungodly, and we suffer despite our righteous response. In 1 Peter 2:18, servants are to be subject "not only to those who are good and considerate but also to those who are crooked." In 3:1, wives are to be subject to their husbands "even if any of them are disobedient to the word."

These two parts of Peter's household code sandwich a central section that speaks of Christ's willingness to do what was right while suffering unjustly (1 Peter 2:21-25) - it is given as an example for us to follow. In the face of unrighteousness, He did not sin, He didn't speak deceitfully, He didn't revile those who reviled Him, and He did not threaten anyone; He simply entrusted Himself to the Father's righteous judgment. This is exactly what we were told to do in Romans 12 - respond to evil with good. He who had all authority

---

1    This a term used to speak of the biblical passages that deal with husbands and wives, parents and children, masters and slaves.

allowed Himself to be treated in an evil manner by evil, tyrannical leaders to whom He had delegated authority, and yet His response was anything but evil.

The linking of this to the household code is abundantly clear by the use of "in the same way" as we transition to wives in 1 Peter 3. And when "in the same way" is repeated to husbands in v.7, although husbands are nowhere in Scripture told to submit to their wives, it is clear that they too must show their submissive heart towards God in responding to unrighteous treatment (in this case, from their wife) with abounding righteousness.

So in the broader context of this passage in 1 Peter, we cannot conclude that an evil Caesar somehow loses his God-delegated authority and that there are no longer any grounds for submission or honor. Instead, we must submit to evil rulers even when they don't do what they are supposed to do.

## SUBMISSION: A RESPONSE TO AUTHORITY

"Wait!" you might now say, "Have you changed your mind? Are you suggesting that we should obey even when they go beyond their delegated authority?" As Paul says several times in Romans, "May it never be!" (Rom 6:1, 15; 7:13). None of this changes the limits of the realm and extent that Caesar has. If he imposes rules he has no authority to impose, then he still has no authority to impose those rules, and we have no duty to submit. Submission is in response to authority - if there is no legitimate authority, how can there be, in that situation, any legitimate submission?

"So what difference does this passage make?" you might ask. This is the point: even if Caesar is evil and tyrannical, regularly imposing rules that he has no authority to make and constantly going beyond his God-delegated limitations, he must still be recognized as God's servant (no matter how badly he is serving), honored as such, and submitted to within the limitations that God gave him. If God can call a tyrant like Nebuchadnezzar "my servant," then I suggest that nobody has the right to say "not my president" (something Americans on both sides of the aisle have said in recent years) if God has given them that position. Being an evil Caesar does not stop someone from being Caesar.

Nebuchadnezzar was God's servant - he was delegated authority to punish the evil that God had found in Israel. They had been evil in their idolatry, and Nebuchadnezzar was God's servant whom He raised up to deal with them. Does that mean that the Babylonians could treat Israel as they wished without limitation? By no means! King Zedekiah was forced to watch his sons murdered, and then his own eyes were gouged out, leaving him with that final, awful image (Jeremiah 39:6-7). Babylon was judged for their treatment of Israel subsequently - as all tyrannical leaders one day will be.

## TRUSTING GOD

Caesar may have no right to tell the church how to conduct worship services and when he does so, he may be rightfully ignored and rebuked, but he does not lose the right to punish evil as a result of his disobedient behavior elsewhere. Even if Caesar is supposed to punish someone who harms you or your loved ones, but he fails to do so, that does not give anyone else the right to take his responsibility upon themselves. Our only recourse then is to continue to entrust ourselves to God (1 Peter 2:23).

"But," you may ask, "didn't Jesus obey tyrannical commands when He was arrested, mistreated, and ultimately went to the cross?" Yes, He did; His time had come. But He also evaded arrest earlier; He also slipped away when they tried to kill Him earlier (e.g., John 8:59). The model that Peter gives us is not one of mindless submission to tyranny but one of a righteous response to unjust suffering while entrusting ourselves to the ultimate judge. There may be times when a righteous response is submissively allowing the mistreatment to occur; there may be other times when a firm "no" is the most righteous and loving response. More on this later.

For now, we must conclude that an evil Caesar is still Caesar, no matter how badly he does his job. Therefore, we must still submit to him regardless, but only to the extent that God has delegated authority to him.

The problem is that evil ruler, almost universally, like to take more authority than they have been delegated. This is the very definition of tyranny. And there are tyrants in every realm where God delegates authority - there are tyrants in the workplace, in the home, in churches, and in government. Tyrants hate those who rebel against them. Yet all tyrants are themselves, ironically, rebels - rebels against the God who has delegated them limited authority that they continually stray beyond.

*"Pilate said to Him, "You do not speak to me? Do You not know that I have authority to release You, and I have authority to crucify You?"*

*Jesus answered, "You would have no authority over Me, unless it had been given you from above; for this reason he who delivered Me to you has the greater sin."* JOHN 19:10-11

# 12

## DECISIONS AND THEIR CONSEQUENCES

In many church circles, "pragmatism" is often a dirty word. And often rightly so. Any compromising of the Word of God under the guise of "the end justifies the means" is wrong. But there is a type of pragmatism that is not in any way unbiblical. And it is this type of pragmatism that we must consider at this stage of our study.

If somebody comes to your house, puts a gun to your head, and demands your wallet, you have limited choices. You can refuse and risk being shot and having your wallet taken; you can comply and give your wallet, and still risk being shot anyway; you could even try fighting back at the risk of being shot and having your wallet taken. However, you would have to inwardly and very quickly weigh up the potential risks and make your decision.

On the other hand, you could also try and explain to the individual with the gun that they had no authority to demand your wallet - that God had not delegated them such authority. Again, I suspect this would not lead the assailant to a life-changing epiphany and a hasty departure. Still, it would most likely lead to you receiving a swift object lesson on the difference between authority and might!

In the same way, when Caesar imposes mandates on the church, and we say "no" because he is making declarations beyond the area where God has delegated authority to him, he is often likely to respond by punishing us. He genuinely believes that he has the authority to do so. It is his job to punish what God calls evil, yet he has determined that something God calls both good and essential is evil. He has punished good - ignoring the "Woe" of Isaiah 5:20 and the inevitable punishment from God. Tyrants will always view any rejection of their self-declared authority to be evil.

We must not confuse authority, which God delegates, and might, which God permits. Just because God has not delegated authority to a person does not mean he has not permitted them to have might. As in the illustration above, the burglar with a gun has no authority over your wallet, but that is not to say that he has no power over it. This distinction is crucial. Just because someone declares authority does not mean they legitimately have any; just because someone doesn't have authority doesn't mean they don't have any power. This is why we need to consider the issue of pragmatism - the reality of the consequences of our decisions.

## ARREST OR VINDICATION?

Many churches have stood their ground over the last two years, and there have been many consequences that have come from it - some have found success in the courts in America, some have been fined, some have been imprisoned. People taking the same stance, for the same reason, in different geographical locations have ended up in very different situations.

This was clearly seen in Canada in the last year. James Coates, of Grace Life Church of Edmonton in Alberta, held church as usual when Caesar had imposed restrictive, tyrannical mandates. He was fined, then arrested. The church continued the following week with somebody else preaching, and so Caesar eventually responded by fencing off the church building. The church's resistance to tyranny led to further tyranny. Eventually, the church decided to go underground - they met in an undisclosed location. Canada, a legacy brand country, had become like China, a communist country. And Canadian Christians, like their Chinese counterparts, had to meet in secret to continue to obey God. That is a pragmatic response to the reality of the consequences of their decisions.

Our church is a short drive from Grace Community Church, where John MacArthur pastors. He very publicly re-opened the church after the initial "15 days to flatten the curve" had dragged into months, defiant of the tyrannical mandates. Because of his high profile and both the church's size and location (Los Angeles County, where the mandates were much stricter), this was big news. What followed was a rollercoaster ride of media interviews, fines, and legal cases. Throughout it, all Pastor John continued to preach faithfully week after week, with an outdoor tent added for those who were more concerned about the virus still. There were fines issued (though never paid), but no arrests were made. The legal battle ended with the state and county paying both parties' legal fees (totaling approximately $2M) and the church continuing just as it had before. MacArthur had taken the same stance as Coates had, but the consequences were very different.

## SMALL CHURCH PRAGMATICS

Fifteen minutes' drive away, our church reopened a week earlier. We are much smaller and not well known. Within a week, a complaint from a snooping neighbor had reached Los Angeles County Health. I had a conversation on the phone with somebody there. He confirmed that we could be in our building to do live stream services - that I, the audio team and the worship team, and those doing various jobs that needed to be done, could be in attendance. Of course, every believer is a minister, and their work is essential, so we had Caesar's permission! But, so I was not misrepresenting our stance, I did end the call by informing him that the doors would remain unlocked and that I had no authority to police those who came in. He understood what I was saying and simply said if there were more complaints, they'd have to follow up.

So each Sunday, we simply held our "live stream service" and got the same attendance as we had before, with as many ministers as wanted to arriving through the unlocked doors. We had social distancing for the service simply because we had sufficient space in our building to use alternate pews. And so we snuck under the radar. Avoidance rather than overt boldness was our approach.

Retrospectively, broadly speaking, I am happy with what we did. Why was it so different than Grace Community Church up the road? Pragmatism. We did what we thought was best for a smaller church with its unique situation. MacArthur deliberately put himself out in front of Caesar as cover for smaller churches such as us - and for that, we were grateful. Yet both churches rejected Caesar's tyranny and sought to obey God and not man; holding services is essential.

## DIFFICULT DECISIONS; DIFFERENT OUTCOMES

The point here is that we have difficult decisions to

make, and there is no guarantee, even if we are faithful, that we will get a positive result, humanly speaking. God-appointed Caesars may be good or evil. Standing up to tyranny may result in honor, or it may result in persecution and harm. The fact that Caesar has been delegated authority by God does not mean we'll be rewarded for good and only punished for evil - the idealism of Romans 13:3 - "Do you want to have no fear of that authority? Do what is good, and you will have praise from the same" - is abundantly clear.

Consider Pharaoh, who was raised up that God might demonstrate His power and proclaim His name through him (Rom 9:17; Ex 9:16) - he was delegated authority as God's servant and yet kept Israel as slaves.

Daniel was rescued from the lions' den (Daniel 6) and his friends from the fiery furnace (Daniel 3). But the apostles were beaten (Acts 5). And, of course, we must consider Christ, who reminded Pilate that the only authority he had was delegated to him by God (John 19:11) before Pilate "delivered him over to them to be crucified" (v16).

So how do we biblically approach this issue of pragmatism while seeking not to compromise in any way?

*"And when they had brought them, they stood them before the Sanhedrin. And the high priest questioned them, saying, "We strictly commanded you not to continue teaching in this name, and yet, you have filled Jerusalem with your teaching and intend to bring this man's blood upon us."*

*But Peter and the apostles answered and said, "We must obey God rather than men." ACTS 5:27-29*

*"For to this you have been called, since Christ also suffered for you, leaving you an example that you should follow in His steps, who did no sin, nor was any deceit found in His mouth; who being reviled, was not reviling in return; while suffering, He was uttering no threats, but kept entrusting Himself to Him who judges righteously." 1 PETER 2:21-23*

# 13

## Two Types of Decisions

We must be clear on a few basic principles: right is right, wrong is wrong, but there are also a lot of things that are neither in and of themselves. There is often a tendency amongst Christians to narrow that middle ground by assigning various options, choices, and behaviors as "good" or "evil" when Scripture doesn't clearly do so.

If someone puts a gun to your head and demands you deny Christ, there is only one option; if they put a gun to your head and demand your wallet, you have many options. These distinctions are important.

We cannot simply dismiss biblical mandates for fear of the pragmatic result of dismissing Caesar's mandates. We cannot dismiss all that the Scripture says about the church, ministry, and meeting together because Caesar has told us to (e.g., Heb 10:25). We have to be obedient regardless of the consequences. Outside of biblical commands, however, we have freedom.

## THE QUAGMIRE OF COVID-19 DECISIONS

In recent months people have had to make many very difficult decisions. Get "vaccinated" or lose your job, or stand up to such impositions legally, or even get a fake "vaccine" card? These moral and ethical dilemmas are hard. Does the use of fetal cell lines make the "vaccines" unacceptable to those who are pro-life? Does the behavior of the Egyptian midwives (Exodus 1:17) and Rahab in Jericho (Joshua 2:1-6) open the door to fake "vaccine" cards? While many would argue one way or another, there are no clear "slam dunk" biblical answers.

People so often want their pastors to make these difficult decisions for them. "Tell me what I should do, pastor!" That is not the pastor's job. They must equip the saints for the work of ministry by the teaching of the Word - they can, and must, lay down the biblical principles that impact such decisions, but where the Scripture is silent, pastors would do well to be silent too. There are consequences that will result from whatever decision is made, and the pastor is not the one who will have to suffer those consequences directly.

As a pastor, it is not my job to tell my church members to be "vaccinated," to wear a mask, or not to wear a mask. If I were to do so, I would be as tyrannical as a Caesar who is trying to impose such things. Legalism is a sin, and I cannot impose mandates on those who attend my church without falling into that sin myself. Nor should we be encouraged to evade the hard work and responsibility of making such choices - wrestling with immovable biblical principles and our ever-changing practical circumstances and prayerfully coming to a decision.

So some will decide to wear a mask when shopping when mandates demand it because, while recognizing Caesar has no such authority, they don't want to deal with any negative consequences; others will decide to stand up to such tyranny and say "No." Some will refuse to mask in stores, but not on planes. Why? Because an argument with the duty manager is not the same thing as being put on a no-fly list! That is pragmatism.

## APOSTLES ARRESTED

This distinction between issues of choice and biblical non-negotiables is seen in Acts 5 when the high priest reminds the apostles that they had been commanded not to teach in the name of Jesus, and yet they had filled Jerusalem with their teaching. In today's era, we'd likely see Christians saying, "We'll just teach in homes" or "We'll only speak to those who want to hear" - a compromise with Caesar would be sought. Yet their response was clear: "We must obey God rather than men" (v29). So in matters where God has spoken, there should be no compromise.

Notice how in the very next verse (v30), they preach at the very people who just told them not to preach. They did not need to do that; it might be argued; they could have left and preached to others in the hope that they found some who wanted to hear. But, no, they preached directly at those who were hostile to their preaching and had told them to stop. They proclaimed Jesus as "leader and savior."

It was a clear statement that their preaching was outside of Caesar's domain - they had another leader to obey. This was a non-negotiable and so much so that they did not merely continue to do it; they did it immediately, to the high priest's face, seemingly as a declaration of their right and responsibility to do so. They did not seek to accommodate Caesar, but rather they declared to him that he was out of his delegated realm.

What a contrast that is with meek submission to Caesar's demands that we have seen so frequently in recent months. He says not to meet, and so churches do not meet; he says meet outside, do not sing, enforce masks, refuse the "unvaccinated," and churches so often comply. It is often as if the apostles' "we must obey God rather than men" has morphed into "we must obey man rather than God" - the subtle approach of statism seems to have blinded us.

The result of the apostles' actions was that the Jewish leaders became furious and intended to kill them (v33). However, due to Gamaliel's counsel (v34-39), they were beaten and released, with the reminder that they were not to "speak in the name of Jesus" (v40). They were punished for doing good.

## RESTING IN GOD'S PROVIDENCE

Doing good should result in praise, and only doing evil should result in punishment. But this is not always, or even often, the case. We must do right even when treated wrongly and trust the consequences to God. This is why pragmatism goes hand in hand with providence.

If we return to 1 Peter 2 and the example of Christ, we see His righteous response - doing good in the face of evil, because He "kept entrusting Himself to Him who judges righteously" (v23). We may get a positive response to doing what the Bible commands, or we may get a negative response, but either way, God is the ultimate judge of all, and He is in control. Jesus knew that, even in the midst of the suffering He endured, His Father could be trusted. And, of course, just as he had Gethsemene beforehand (Luke 22:39-46), so we too must cry out to Him in prayer as we entrust ourselves to Him.

On this issue, our hearts must be settled. Righteous living will always lead to some form of suffering (2 Tim 3:12), and so we must be prepared to endure and trust God with the outcome. Our only concern is to be obedient to His Word.

The apostles understood this and rejoiced that they'd "been considered worthy to suffer shame for the Name" (Acts 5:41). And, of course, they continued "teaching and proclaiming the good news that Jesus is the Christ" (v42). They obeyed and trusted the results to God. Whether the outcome is, humanly speaking, good or not, God always remains good.

Equally, when we make decisions that are neither biblical nor unbiblical, we need not be concerned by the outcome. It's not as if we can choose an option and be wrong if the Bible allows us to choose either. We cannot believe that God could somehow be surprised by our decision. Yes, the decision can have significant consequences, but we must trust in God's sovereignty.

So we have difficult decisions to make. Of course, we must obey God, not men, but the degree to which we react to the tyrannical overreach is often down to our own choice, with no clear right or wrong biblically. And the consequences of these decisions may be huge. So how do we make such difficult decisions?

*Therefore it is necessary to be in subjection, not only because of that wrath, but also because of conscience. For because of this you also pay taxes, for rulers are servants of God, devoting themselves to this very thing. Render to all what is due them: tax to whom tax is due; custom to whom custom; fear to whom fear; honor to whom honor. Owe nothing to anyone except to love one another; for he who loves his neighbor has fulfilled the law.*

*For this, "You shall not commit adultery, You shall not murder, You shall not steal, You shall not covet," and if there is any other commandment, it is summed up in this word, "You shall love your neighbor as yourself."*

*Love does not work evil against a neighbor; therefore love is the fulfillment of the Law.* ROMANS 13:5-10

*"Now accept the one who is weak in faith, but not for the purpose of passing judgment on opinions. One person has faith that he may eat all things, but he who is weak eats vegetables only. The one who eats must not view the one who does not eat with contempt, and the one who does not eat must not judge the one who eats, for God accepted him.*

*Who are you to judge the servant of another? To his own master he stands or falls; and he will stand, for the Lord is able to make him stand. One person judges one day above another, another regards every day alike. Each person must be fully convinced in his own mind."* ROMANS 14:1-6

# 14

## Motivated by Love and Directed by Conscience

Romans 13 has been the key passage we have looked at in regards to the interaction between Caesar and the Church. We started out with the erroneous interpretation that is so widely held - "obey Caesar unless sin" - and, after looking at the foundational biblical principles, we took a deeper dive into the passage, including the crucial preceding context.

Now, as we continue on through Romans 13, which has presented a very idealistic picture of how government should function, it leads us to a broader focus on how we should behave, particularly with regards to how we treat our fellow believers.

Though it goes beyond the scope of this deliberately brief book to take as deep a dive as we did earlier in Romans 13, it is clear enough to see two key themes developed in the second half of chapter 13 and into chapter 14 - love and conscience.

## LOVE

The theme of loving one another is found throughout Scripture, though it is no coincidence that it is also found immediately after our passage on God's delegated exercising of vengeance in Romans 13.

In Romans 13:7, we are to render to each person what is due to them - the references to tax, fear, custom, and honor are a bridge leading us out of the context of Caesar and into the broader context of treating our fellow believers in an appropriate manner. Verse 8 then builds on this requirement of giving what is due to each person by telling us to "owe nothing to anyone except to love one another." Verse 9 makes it clear that love involves obedience to God - doing what He calls good. "Love does not work evil against a neighbor" (v10).

When God's word is clear, then our course of action is equally so. But when we have the liberty to choose, then we must always be motivated by love - whenever we love, as God defines it, we are in obedience to God.

So we should have the mind of Christ, who considered others more important than Himself, when we make decisions (Phil 2:1-5). This is especially so within the church, amongst our brothers and sisters in Christ. Self must be put aside, and the good of others must take precedent.

Doing what God commands us to do and not doing what He commands us not to is both loving and good - to Him and to those around us. But as much as good must be defined by God, so must love. Therefore, in seeking to love, we must be cautious not to allow love to be defined for us by unbelievers. Too often, the enemy of God will say to us, "love your neighbor," when they really mean, "you must agree with me and comply with Caesar like I am."

So while we must honor Caesar in the realm which God has delegated to him, if he steps outside of his realm, he is not to be honored for that. Sometimes honor is merited and sometimes not - "what is due" is a crucial caveat (v7). But love is always due.

## CONSCIENCE

As we move from Romans 13 to chapter 14, we move from the general requirement to love one another to a more specific way of doing so. One issue in this section of the letter is "passing judgment on opinions" (14:1) - matters that we are neither commanded nor forbidden to do.

Some believers are weak in their faith (v1) and feel convicted that they must not do something that they are actually free in Christ to do - Paul uses the illustration of a vegetarian diet here (v2-3). Now, this is not an issue of health but of righteousness - the person abstaining believes it would be wrong for them to do otherwise. It is clear biblically that they can, in fact, eat meat without sinning - it is a weakness in faith that hinders them (v2). What is clear is that those who eat differently in this regard must accept one another (v1) and have no contempt for each other (v3). In these areas where we have a choice, we must not judge one another (v4, 10). The important thing is to live our life for Christ (v6-8), to whom we must ultimately give an account (v12).

If we are convicted not to take a particular path, then we must not (v22-23), even if it is an outworking of our weakness. Of course, we must not put down permanent foundations on non-biblical issues - as we grow in faith, we may well change our minds. We want to mature into an ever-stronger faith.

The key point is that there is freedom for us to disagree on this type of issue without contempt or judgment. We must not tear down the work of God for the sake of such things (v20)

## PRACTICAL OUTWORKINGS

So let us consider the issue of masks, for example. Again, I'm no doctor and won't comment on the efficacy or otherwise of various masks, but when Caesar says you have to wear one, he has strayed out of his God delegated boundaries.

If you believe that the mask is an effective way of preventing the transmission of a virus, you might decide that wearing one is a harmless way to protect your neighbor from potentially getting sick, and thus you may well choose to wear one, even though Caesar's imposition is unwarranted. However, if you think that the efficacy of the mask is negligible and thus that its imposition is a form of compelled speech (akin to being forced to wear a T-shirt with a message you don't agree with), then you are likely to refuse to do so.

The wearing of a mask is not a biblical issue per se. You cannot turn to Hezekiah 34:23 and see a command to "mask up when Caesar says so!" Thus we have the freedom to choose. The biblical issues here are that, firstly, Caesar has no authority delegated to him to be our doctor and make medical decisions for us - he is to punish evil as God declares it, not declare right and wrong merely as he sees fit. Secondly, whatever decision we make must be motivated by love and our conscience.

With regards to love, it means that if we don't wear a mask, it is not merely because it's uncomfortable, we can't be bothered, or we're just prone to argue. Rather it comes from a heart of love - that our non-compliance to Caesar's tyrannical mandates comes from seeking the best of others in combination with our conviction that to bow to that mandate would be wrong. Perhaps our concern for others is the loss of freedom within society in the future, or merely the misrepresentation of Caesar's delegated realm through compliance; the point, either way, is that our motivation is not selfish and seeks to serve Christ.

Equally, if we do wear a mask, it is not merely to fit in or to avoid conflict but is genuinely wrought from our conscience and desire to love others - a belief that doing so is making a positive difference to others around us. Nonetheless, there should be a conscious understanding that this is our choice and not Caesar's enforcement.

Either way, if we, as Christians, disagree on such matters - on how we should conduct ourselves in this strange world - there should be no place for judgment or contempt. We may well come to different decisions on such matters, and that is ok. In particular, those stronger in faith should take care not to pass judgment on the weak but rather to accept them as they live in accordance with their own conscience before God, who will judge their hearts.

*"See to it that no one takes you captive through philosophy and empty deception, according to the tradition of men, according to the elementary principles of the world, and not according to Christ...*

*If you have died with Christ to the elementary principles of the world, why, as if you were living in the world, do you submit yourself to decrees: "Do not handle, nor taste, nor touch"?*

*Which deal with everything destined to perish with use, which are in accordance with the commands and teachings of men; which are matters having, to be sure, a word of wisdom in self-made religion and self-abasement and severe treatment of the body, but are of no value against fleshly indulgence."* COLOSSIANS 2:8, 20-23

# 15

## Legalism and the Sufficiency of Scripture

As we continue looking at how to deal with these decisions that are not determined directly from Scripture, we turn to the issue of legalism.

To be clear, while some use the term "legalism" to speak of works-based salvation (keeping laws to be saved), I am using it to speak of the imposition of rules and behavior that the Bible itself does not impose as if the doing of such things were sinful.

Paul deals with this sort of legalism in Colossians 2. In verse 8, he warns his readers not to allow anyone to "take them captive through philosophy and empty deception according to the traditions of men, according to the elemental principles, and not according to Christ." There are ways of thinking that are deceptive and fruitless. These come, not of Christ, but of the hearts and minds of men and demons.

He speaks of two such ways. Firstly, there are those who make claims of visions and angelic worship, though, in reality, they are "puffed up for nothing" by their "fleshy mind" (v18). Secondly, there is legalism - Paul uses the examples of insisting on specific days of worship and dietary rules (v16,21). These two false philosophies, while seeming very different at first glance, have one common thread. Whether you need dreams and visions or additional rules, you are saying that Christ is somehow not enough. It is a two-headed beast - a rejection of the sufficiency of Christ and His Word.

Legalism is ultimately in harmony with the devil and the traditions of men, but it is not of Christ. If, through our union with Christ by faith, we have died to these demonic powers, why would we embrace legalism (v20-21)? This is no minor matter, but rather a way of life that is apart from Christ.

This is why when we impose rules Christ has not imposed, this "self-abasement" does not make us more godly, as its adherents might claim, but actually has "no value against fleshly indulgences" (v23). It may have the appearance of wisdom, but ironically, legalists are not more spiritually mature but are, in fact, weaker in their faith.

## LEGALISM IN CHURCH

When I say in our worship service, "Let's stand and

sing!" I am not implying that if you sit and contemplate the lyrics quietly that you are in some way sinning. It is a general request to the church, but each individual can decide how to worship, assuming they don't hinder the worship of others. If I were to go over and rebuke someone for worshipping silently, I would be going beyond the limits of my authority. That would be legalism.

In the same way, when churches take orders from Caesar, they not only give away the authority that has been delegated to them, but they also stumble into legalism. As a pastor of a church, I cannot tell people they must wear a mask to come in any more than I could tell women not to wear pants[1] or men that they are obliged to wear suits to attend. Even if such a mandate was from my own heart, rather than being passed down by a tyrannical Caesar, such imposition has no biblical warrant and would be a form of legalism. Like Caesar, I would be a tyrannical leader going beyond the limits of the authority I have been delegated.

Legalism's imposition of extra-Biblical rules and regulations is loved by tyrants who crave more power and is tolerated, and often embraced, by those under such leadership because we are prone to fear of grey areas. We often want to be told "this is right, and this is wrong" in every single area of life, ridding ourselves of the responsibility of making decisions and navigating

1   That's" trousers" to my fellow Brits!

such grey areas prayerfully.

It should therefore be no surprise to us if we see that churches that have historically been prone to legalism are often the same churches that saw no problem with imposing Caesar's mandates upon their churches. Those who would separate the "vaccinated" from the "unvaccinated," those who would impose mask mandates - these are often the same ones that had made extra-biblical impositions long before any of us had heard of Covid-19. After all, if a pastor has constantly gone beyond the limits of their delegated authority, why would they begrudge Caesar from doing the same?

Many might say concerning such churches that these overreaches are frustrating and ill-informed or even outright sinful, but they aren't heretical. It is not as if they deny the deity of Christ! That is, of course, true. To be sure, this is no major heresy. But that is not to say that it is not significant.

Legalism is wicked. It gives the impression of godliness when it is, in reality, a rejection of Christ's sufficiency. It can act as a cover for other sins. And in this scenario, it is a handing over of pastors' authority that was delegated and entrusted to them to Caesar in an act of mutiny - whether this was a conscious decision or whether they were blinded by the gradual encroachment of statism. This is no minor thing - legalism is a serious issue

One of the blessings of Covid-19 has been how it has exposed so many things that were previously hidden away - fear of death, a laissez-faire attitude towards church and meeting with the saints for equipping and ministry, a greater desire for comfort than holiness, and also a tolerance for legalism.

*"Then it [government] should not ... turn against the nation's religious beliefs that only intensify in times of epidemics. Rather, when God's judgments break out the government ought to share in the spirit of awe that stirs the souls before the majesty of God. Rather than prohibiting prayer services it should itself proclaim a day of prayer. In this way its solemn decisions and actions will underscore the impression that as a government it is powerless to ward off the plague that is visiting the nation and that it knows no better refuge for deliverance than to humble itself before almighty God."*

ABRAHAM KUYPER, *Our Program: A Christian Political Manifesto*, 1879

*"Now, if ever, is the time for the church to assert its sovereignty over against encroachments by the state. The church is in sacred duty bound to rise up in majesty and proclaim to the world that it enjoys freedom of worship, not by the grace of the state, but as a God-given right; and that it preaches the Word of God, not by the grace of human governments, but solely at the command of the sovereign God and its sovereign King, seated at God's right hand."*

R.B. KUIPER, *The Glorious Body Of Christ*, 1967

*"The doctrine of forfeiture maintains that it is normally the Christian duty to submit to God-ordained authorities. However, if authorities blatantly transgress the parameters God has established for them - if they move outside of their lawful authority as designed by God. Then they forfeit the right to submission."*

DAVID W. HALL, *Savior or Servant? Putting Government In Its Place*, 2020

*"Authentic Christians cannot allow either majority opinion or government edicts to determine what we believe, especially at this moment in history."*

JOHN MACARTHUR, *"Facing COVID-19 Without Fear"*, 2021

# Conclusion

"But someone came and reported to them, "The men whom you put in prison are standing in the temple and teaching the people!"

Then the captain went along with the officers and proceeded to bring them back without violence (for they were afraid of the people, that they might be stoned).

And when they had brought them, they stood them before the Sanhedrin. And the high priest questioned them, saying, "We strictly commanded you not to continue teaching in this name, and yet, you have filled Jerusalem with your teaching and intend to bring this man's blood upon us."

But Peter and the apostles answered and said, "We must obey God rather than men. The God of our fathers raised up Jesus, whom you put to death by hanging Him on a tree. This One God exalted to His right hand as a Leader and a Savior, to grant repentance to Israel, and forgiveness of sins. And we are witnesses of these things, and so is the Holy Spirit, whom God gave to those who obey Him."
ACTS 5:25-32

# The God-Given, Limited, Delegated Authority of Caesar

In this study, we have clearly seen what authority Caesar has been delegated by God. He is God's servant rewarding good and punishing evil, as defined by God. When Caesar does this, he is the right person, exercising his delegated authority in the right realm, to the right extent. Our duty is to submit to him as he ministers as a servant of God. But when he goes beyond these boundaries, he has no authority because the only authority he does have is from God (Rom 13:2).

If I came to your house and looked at your red couch and said, "This is disgraceful! Disgusting! Get yourself a blue couch immediately!" I hope your response would be to tell me to mind my own business before slinging me out of your house. Not my house, not my realm, not my decision, not my business; no authority. It's your house, your realm, your decision, your business; you have the authority.

When Christians isolate Romans 13:1 from its context, they come to the wrong conclusions regarding the extent of Caesar's authority, and the common misinterpretation that we addressed at the beginning of this book is allowed to prosper unchallenged. It is falsely presumed that Caesar can make up whatever rules he likes (statism), and our only exemption is if obedience would cause us to sin. In such an unbiblical model of government, Caesar could tell us to do anything that he wanted, and we would be obliged to submit in almost every case.

We then permissively allow Caesar, in a manner of speaking, to come into our home and rearrange the furniture, destroying and replacing whatever he wants, and then send us the bill, no doubt. When any leader (of any realm) goes beyond their God-given purpose and limits, they are entering into tyranny. Tyrannical husbands, tyrannical parents, tyrannical employers, and tyrannical pastors are all in opposition to God as much as tyrannical Caesars.

## TYRANNY AND COVID

During this time of COVID, Caesar has come to God's entrusted leaders of His church and said in effect, "God said meeting together is good, but for now it is evil, and you must not do it, or I will punish you. For how long?

15 days. No, one month. No, six months. No, a year. But eventually, you can meet, but only outside your building, not inside. And when you do meet outside, I will tell you what you must wear, how close to each other you may stand (don't you dare greet one another with a holy kiss!), and, again, I will punish you if you don't comply. Oh, and when you meet outside, wearing your compulsory clothing, sufficiently far apart from one another, you cannot sing either!"

In this scenario, Caesar has no more right to intrude upon the outworking of the worship of God than Uzziah did (2 Chronicles 26) - he is not God's chosen leader in that realm. God has delegated different leaders for the church. Caesar has no authority there.

More so, even outside the church, when we go to grocery stores, restaurants, and the like, Caesar has limited authority. He cannot make up whatever rules he likes and mete out punishment for not keeping them. His role is limited to the punishment of evil and the rewarding of good. He is not our healthcare provider; he is not our educator; he is not our guardian, nor our mentor; he is not our best friend, and in practice, rarely, if ever, does he have our best interests at heart. He is not our conscience; he is not the discerner of good and evil; he is not our parent; and, in the most definitive terms, he is not our god. Instead, he is God's servant and, to a lesser extent, ours.

Sadly, years of unbridled statism have emboldened

Caesar. The degree to which countries have embraced tyrannical oversight during the last two years has mirrored the degree to which statism was previously accepted. Citizens had been trained to look to Caesar as their educator and protect them from false information, as their doctor to keep them healthy, as their moral authority to tell them what is right and what is wrong. No wonder, in the midst of a declared crisis, Caesar is looked to as the people's savior who must be trusted and obeyed.

Again, it should be of little surprise that when unbelievers have purged God from society that such statism should arise more and more. What is more disappointing is when Christians, who claim that God is the one who defines good and evil and is their only savior, lock arms with those who reject their faith - together, they elevate Caesar into a role that God did not give him and one that, in many ways, replaces God.

In a similar way, while it is wrong when Christians embrace statism in society at large, it is far worse when this idolatrous doctrine crosses over the threshold of God's church. I know that so many churches have embraced this with the very best intentions, but that does not negate the result or the impact. The message to such tyranny from God's people should be united, bold, and unapologetic - "We reject your authority. We reject your impositions. We reject your mandates."

That is not to say that a church leader cannot agree

with Caesar. For example, if Caesar were to say, "You should sing "In Christ Alone" at least once a month in your services," that does not mean you are now forbidden from doing so. You may well have wanted to do that anyway. And so you can. But be sure to understand that in doing so, you are not complying with Caesar's tyrannical mandates, you are simply doing what you wanted to do anyway, and your desires happen to coincide. A broken clock is right twice a day, as the saying goes, and Caesar may on occasion want you to do things that you also want to do. Agreement is not submission.

Also, note that none of this has anything to do with the efficacy (or lack thereof) of masks or "vaccines" - Christians can hold different views on such matters and make different decisions. What we are concluding here from our study of Scripture is simply to do with the purpose and limitations of human authority. Caesar does not have the authority delegated to him to decide what you wear and what you inject yourself with, but if you happen to agree with his conclusions in these regards, then go ahead and do these things. Just please refrain from calling your agreement compliance.

## Concluding Exhortations

I want to end by saying a few things in conclusion to three different groups of people: those who trust in Christ, church leaders, and Caesar himself.

## TO THOSE OF US WHO BELONG TO CHRIST

We are to submit to all governing authorities - if authority has been delegated to that person, in that realm, and they are ruling according to the purposes and limitations God has given. By submitting to them, we are submitting to God, who has delegated to them the authority that they are operating in. More so, we should fear not submitting, for rebellion against them is rebellion against God whose authority they are exercising.

This is, however, not a call to blanket obedience to any and all civil government. If somebody tells us we have to obey them, our questions must be who are they, what authority has God delegated to them, in what realm were they granted authority, and what are God's purposes and limits in the authority He has delegated to them.

When Jesus turned the tables over in the temple, the question He was asked was regarding His authority (John 2:18). The issue of authority is the crucial one. Not "why do you do it?", but "on what authority do you do it?"

So we are to submit when somebody is exercising legitimate, God-delegated authority, but when someone tells us to submit, we should not automatically assume that they have legitimate authority. With regards to Caesar specifically, he has authority to punish evil as defined by God - he is not our parent, nor our doctor, far less our God. We render unto Caesar what is Caesar's, but he does not get to decide what is his; God does.

When he steps out of his delegated authority and behaves as if he is a god, the church must arise and warn him of his violation. For the church to bow before his demands is not only tantamount to idolatry, but it is also unloving to both Caesar (who is emboldened in his tyrannical demands and thus further entrenched in God's judgment) and to those who continue in their ungodly worship of him. We are, for all intents and purposes, endorsing his tyrannical reign.

When Daniel's friends were asked who would save them from the fiery furnace, they responded by saying that God was able, but "if not, let it be known to you, O king, that we are not going to serve your gods, and we will not worship the golden image that you have set up" (Daniel 3:18). They were willing to go to death rather than comply with Caesar. Are we prepared to deny ourselves, take up our cross and follow Him? Or are we more interested in a comfortable and peaceful existence?

## To The Local Church and Its Leaders

If God has delegated authority over a local church to you, do not cede that authority to another whom God has not granted authority in this realm. To do so is to bow before Caesar as if God had made him your good shepherd under whose authority you serve; as if he were your god.

Many people have (rightly) left churches over this very issue, and so believers are being forced to separate into two groups - those who bow before Caesar and those who obey God and not men (Acts 5).

Here in Los Angeles County, California, there are churches that criticized and condemned those who boldly resisted Caesar's tyranny. These churches that shut down, met outside, enforced masks and social distancing, banned singing - often all at once - are now meeting indoors without restrictions again - not because the threat has changed (other indoor areas still have mask mandates here), but because the very people they criticized forced this issue through the courts until there was a Supreme Court ruling. The Supreme Court ruling clearly showed that the restrictions were always illegal here under the Constitution.

Yet I have not come across a single example of any of these church leaders repenting or even apologizing to those whom they criticized. They are slow in admitting their error but quick in benefitting from those they spoke out against.

If this is how American churches responded, what hope was there for churches in nations without such a robust constitution protecting their right to practice their faith? What we must all understand, whatever country we reside in, is that the U.S. Constitution is not granting Americans any rights per se. It is simply recognizing rights that God has given them and preventing Caesar from taking those rights away. Thus these are rights that belong to all, regardless of nationality, as we have seen. If American churches, whose constitution protects their God-given rights, fold under pressure from lesser Caesars, what hope is there for those in countries where the ultimate Caesar does not recognize those God-given rights?

So many of those with the best opportunity to stand up to Caesar's tyranny have chosen to bow before him. The only way forward for these churches is to get a biblical understanding of authority and repent, publicly declaring their error and not bowing before him again.

## TO CAESARS—ALL THOSE WITH GOD-DELEGATED AUTHORITY IN THE CIVIL REALM

Caesar needs to be told very clearly, by as many churches and Christians as possible, acting like the priests in the time of Uzziah, to "Get out of the sanctuary, for you have been unfaithful and will have no honor from Yahweh God." (2 Chr 26:18b). Though the type of Caesars we have are, no matter how bad they are, delegated by our sovereign God and perhaps even a way of God dealing with us, that does not make them immune to judgment. "Woe to Assyria, the rod of My anger and the staff in whose hands is My indignation" - this alone makes that clear (Isa 10:5). Verse

11 makes it even clearer - "So it will be that when the Lord has completed all His work on Mount Zion and on Jerusalem, He will say, "I will punish the fruit of the arrogant heart of the king of Assyria and the pomp of his eyes which are raised high." Tyrannical Caesars will one day be judged.

Isaiah 5:20-21 gives them another woe - "Woe to those who call evil good and good evil,

Who substitute darkness for light and light for darkness, who substitute bitter for sweet and sweet for bitter! Woe to those who are wise in their own eyes and understanding in their own sight!"

We had already noted verse 20 and its echo in Romans 12:9, but look at verse 21's warning about them being wise in their own eyes and see a similar echo in Romans 12:16's "Do not be wise in your own eyes."

All who are granted a position in civil government, from law enforcement officers through judges and governors to presidents and prime ministers, must be humble, acknowledging the God who has appointed them to be His servant. They must recognize that their duty is to reward good and punish evil and that it is God alone who gets to define those terms. They must understand that their position brings incredible responsibility and that they will be judged more strictly as a result. For every time they call good evil and evil good, for every time they punish good or reward evil, for every time they go beyond the role God gave them, they will be held accountable.

May God grant them the same mercy He showed Nebuchadnezzar, whom He made into a beast that He might be brought to humility and repentance before his life was over (Daniel 4)!

May those kings who stand against Yahweh and His Anointed (Psalm 2:2), wanting to tear down His legitimate authority over them (v.3), know that He laughs at them (v.4) and speaks to them in His anger (v5). May they heed His warning (v10), serve Him "with fear and rejoice with trembling" (v11)! May they "kiss the Son, lest He becomes angry," and they "perish in the way" (v12a)! May his wrath towards them be atoned for as they find their refuge in Him(v12b)!

One thing is sure: whether they repent or not, God who appointed them will be glorified through them.

AMEN!